UNHOLY TRICKS

Also by Terence Reese and David Bird

MIRACLES OF CARD PLAY

Unholy Tricks

More Miraculous Card Play

TERENCE REESE and DAVID BIRD

LONDON
VICTOR GOLLANCZ LTD
in association with Peter Crawley
1984

First published in Great Britain 1984
by Victor Gollancz Ltd,
14 Henrietta Street, London WC2E 8QJ

© Terence Reese and David Bird 1984

FOREWORD

Some of the stories in this book have appeared in bridge magazines around the world. Our thanks are due to the editors of *Bridge Magazine*, *Bridge World* (USA) and *International Popular Bridge Monthly* for permission to reprint.

Once again, I must make it clear that the original stories were written by David Bird alone. One reviewer of our first collection regretted the practice of adding a 'famous' name to the masthead, simply to promote sales. I need hardly add that this is not my style. Discerning readers will be able to spot the places where I have left my mark.

TERENCE REESE

British Library Cataloguing in Publication Data
Reese, Terence
  Unholy tricks.
  1. Contract bridge
  I. Title II. Bird, David, *1946–*
  795.41'5   GV1282.3

ISBN 0–575–03493–9

Photoset and printed in Great Britain by
Photobooks (Bristol) Ltd.

Contents

At the Monastery of St. Titus

The Abbot:	A capable but uninspired player; greatly jealous of his reputation.
Brother Lucius:	The monastery's chief accountant and its most cunning and deceptive card player.
Brother Xavier:	Monastery barber for the past twenty years; an admirer of Brother Lucius and a good player.
Brother Anthony:	Member of the silent Eustacian order and therefore, of necessity, an over-cautious bidder.
Brother Aelred:	The monastery organist; a weak but aspiring player.
Brother Damien:	A promising postulant, keen to make his mark on the monastery bridge scene.
Brother Paulo:	An Italian monk transferred to St. Titus to strengthen the monastery first team.

In the African Jungle

Brother Tobias:	A missionary who has successfully converted the Bozwambi tribe to the Acol system.
Brother Luke:	Right-hand man of Brother Tobias, but his keenest rival at the table.
The Witch-doctor:	A wild overbidder, much feared by the other natives who never dare double him.
Mbozi:	Docile and lazy during the play of the hand but extremely fierce in the post-mortem.
Mrs. Okoku:	Captain of the Bozwambi Ladies team and a sturdy player.
Miss Nabooba:	A slender 19-year old who shows rare promise at the game.

PART I

At the Monastery of St. Titus

1

Brother Aelred's Birthday Present

Brother Aelred patted his hair into position, straightened his cassock rope and stepped into the Abbot's study. "You sent for me, Abbot?" he said.

"Ah, Brother Aelred. I understand from the janitor that some wine arrived for you yesterday morning."

"A few bottles of Volnay, Abbot, that's all. A birthday present from my uncle in Worthing. I trust I haven't infringed any regulations."

"It's not a matter of regulations," declared the Abbot. "At St. Titus we believe in sharing our possessions."

"Very well, Abbot," said Brother Aelred with a neutral expression. "I'll bring the case of wine to supper tonight and everyone can have half a glass."

The Abbot sighed. "Perhaps that's not such a good idea," he said. "Most of our brethren wouldn't know a good Volnay from Brother Michael's second-pressing blackberry." He paused to consider the matter. "I tell you what. Leave three bottles in my cell and we'll say no more about it."

"Are you sure, Abbot?" said Brother Aelred. "That's very good of you."

"Well, it's fitting that so generous a gift should be properly appreciated," replied the Abbot.

An hour or two later the Abbot had finished his paperwork for the day. After checking that the three bottles had been delivered to his cell, he headed for the main cardroom. He was soon involved in a lively £1 game.

E–W game, dealer South

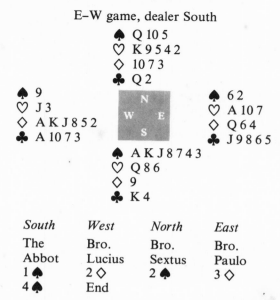

♠ Q 10 5
♡ K 9 5 4 2
◇ 10 7 3
♣ Q 2

♠ 9
♡ J 3
◇ A K J 8 5 2
♣ A 10 7 3

♠ 6 2
♡ A 10 7
◇ Q 6 4
♣ J 9 8 6 5

♠ A K J 8 7 4 3
♡ Q 8 6
◇ 9
♣ K 4

South	West	North	East
The	Bro.	Bro.	Bro.
Abbot	Lucius	Sextus	Paulo
1 ♠	2 ◇	2 ♠	3 ◇
4 ♠	End		

Brother Lucius led the ace of diamonds against four spades and continued with the king. The Abbot ruffed and then led ♣ 4 with a casual air.

Brother Lucius, alert as ever, was quick to go in with the ace. This could hardly cost if declarer held ♣ K x x and might be essential if he held ♣ K x. To play low might allow declarer to eliminate diamonds and trumps and exit in clubs, forcing West to open the heart suit.

Brother Lucius exited with a second round of clubs, won in hand by declarer. The Abbot now crossed to the queen of trumps and ruffed the last diamond. West had shown good values already, so the Abbot decided to play East for the ace of hearts. He crossed to dummy's ten of trumps and led a low heart to the queen.

Brother Lucius unblocked his jack of hearts on this trick, and his partner was able to capture the next two heart tricks, putting the contract one down.

"Oh, what bad luck, Abbot," said Brother Sextus. "If Lucius hadn't happened to play that jack of hearts, it seems you'd have made it."

"The jack was nearest my thumb," observed Brother Lucius with a bland smile.

"That was fortunate for you," declared the Abbot, unamused. "I didn't expect to make it, anyhow. I was bidding defensively."

"Yes, we had a good fit our way," said Brother Lucius. "On a spade lead five diamonds is only broken by a heart switch at trick 2."

"Automatic with that club suit in the dummy," declared the Abbot. "Shall we continue?"

The next rubber saw the Abbot partnering Brother Paulo.

Game all, dealer West

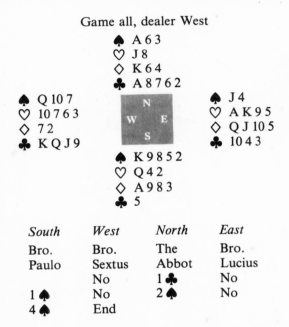

```
                    ♠ A 6 3
                    ♡ J 8
                    ♢ K 6 4
                    ♣ A 8 7 6 2
 ♠ Q 10 7                          ♠ J 4
 ♡ 10 7 6 3         N              ♡ A K 9 5
 ♢ 7 2          W       E          ♢ Q J 10 5
 ♣ K Q J 9          S              ♣ 10 4 3
                    ♠ K 9 8 5 2
                    ♡ Q 4 2
                    ♢ A 9 8 3
                    ♣ 5
```

South	West	North	East
Bro.	Bro.	The	Bro.
Paulo	Sextus	Abbot	Lucius
	No	1♣	No
1♠	No	2♠	No
4♠	End		

Brother Paulo, who had been bidding somewhat gaily all evening, arrived in a wafer-thin spade game. The king of clubs lead was won in dummy and a heart played towards the queen. Brother Lucius, sitting East, went in with the king and switched to the queen of diamonds.

Brother Paulo won in dummy and cleared his heart trick. After winning the diamond return, he discarded dummy's last diamond on the queen of hearts. These cards remained:

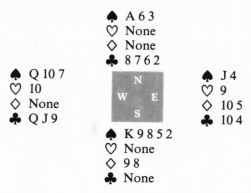

```
                    ♠ A 6 3
                    ♡ None
                    ◇ None
                    ♣ 8 7 6 2
    ♠ Q 10 7                              ♠ J 4
    ♡ 10              N                    ♡ 9
    ◇ None         W     E                ◇ 10 5
    ♣ Q J 9          S                    ♣ 10 4
                    ♠ K 9 8 5 2
                    ♡ None
                    ◇ 9 8
                    ♣ None
```

Declarer led a diamond and West ruffed with the 7. Brother Paulo paused for thought. If West were ruffing from a doubleton trump, it seemed there was no way to make the contract. But what if West had three trumps?

Realising that to overruff would leave him with two losers, Brother Paulo discarded a club from dummy. The contract was now secure. Declarer ruffed the club exit, drew trumps in two rounds and ruffed his remaining diamond.

"You were a bit light for your jump to game, weren't you," queried the Abbot.

"If you don't lift ze hammer, you don't crack ze nut," replied Brother Paulo, humming to himself as he totted up the rubber.

"I make it you had a 9-count with a singleton in my suit," persisted the Abbot, studying the ruddy-faced Brother Paulo closely. "Have you been drinking?"

"As it happens, yes," replied Brother Paulo. "I had a glass or two of most excellent claret in Brother Aelred's cell before ze game."

"Claret?" exclaimed the Abbot, wincing visibly. "Volnay is a burgundy, for heaven's sake. I'd have thought even an Italian would know that."

"We were drinking Chateau Camensac," said Brother Paulo, smiling at the memory. "Most delicious, it was. His uncle did send him some Volnay too, but apparently it was 1975. A disastrous vintage, fit only for cooking. Do you make the rubber 14 points?"

2

The Arrival of Padre Giotto

Brother Paulo had always maintained close links with his previous monastery, that of San Giovanni Battista in northern Italy. For some months he had been planning a visit of some Italian monks to St. Titus. The purpose was twofold – to increase the spiritual bond between the two establishments, and to arrange a series of team-of-four matches.

"Didn't I tell you the train would be late?" grunted the Abbot, stamping his feet on the platform in an attempt to ward off the cold. "Ah, at last. This must be their train."

The train ground to a halt and the white-cassocked monks spilled out of the carriage, expressing their delight at seeing Brother Paulo again. The Abbot watched with distaste as Brother Paulo embraced his former colleagues.

"Abbot," said Brother Paulo proudly, "allow me to introduce you to Padre Giotto, Abbot of San Giovanni."

"Aha! Sir Hugo!" said the Padre, walking towards the Abbot with his arms outstretched. The Abbot gritted his teeth as Padre Giotto gave him a garlic-loaded embrace, kissing him on both cheeks.

"We are most looking forwards to ze bridge matches against San Titus," said Padre Giotto, flashing his perfect white teeth. "Brother Paulo and I will renew our old partnering. I hope he has not forgetted the system!"

"Brother Paulo is a St. Titus man now," said the Abbot firmly. "He will be partnering Brother Lucius as usual."

After a hearty supper washed down by some San Giovanni red wine that the Italians had brought with them, the first match started.

Love all, dealer South

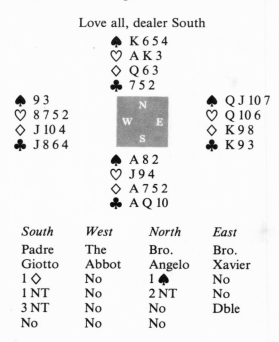

	♠ K 6 5 4	
	♡ A K 3	
	◇ Q 6 3	
	♣ 7 5 2	

♠ 9 3		♠ Q J 10 7
♡ 8 7 5 2		♡ Q 10 6
◇ J 10 4		◇ K 9 8
♣ J 8 6 4		♣ K 9 3

	♠ A 8 2	
	♡ J 9 4	
	◇ A 7 5 2	
	♣ A Q 10	

South	West	North	East
Padre	The	Bro.	Bro.
Giotto	Abbot	Angelo	Xavier
1 ◇	No	1 ♠	No
1 NT	No	2 NT	No
3 NT	No	No	Dble
No	No	No	

Bearing in mind the limited nature of the opponents' auction, Brother Xavier decided to ask for the lead of dummy's first bid suit by doubling three no-trumps. The Abbot dutifully opened the nine of spades.

Padre Giotto held off the first trick and won the spade continuation in dummy. A finesse of the ten of clubs lost to the jack and the Abbot switched to the jack of diamonds. Declarer let this hold and ducked again when the Abbot followed with the diamond ten. He won the third round of diamonds, crossed to the king of hearts and finessed the club queen. Then he cashed the ace of clubs, arriving at this end position:

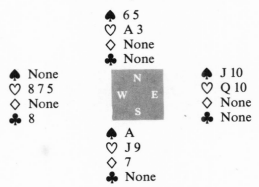

```
              ♠ 6 5
              ♡ A 3
              ◇ None
              ♣ None
♠ None                      ♠ J 10
♡ 8 7 5        N            ♡ Q 10
◇ None      W     E         ◇ None
♣ 8            S            ♣ None
              ♠ A
              ♡ J 9
              ◇ 7
              ♣ None
```

When Padre Giotto cashed the last diamond, throwing a heart from dummy, East discarded the ten of hearts. Declarer now scored the ace of hearts, ace of spades and jack of hearts for his contract.

"Sorry, partner," said the Abbot heavily.

"What do you mean?" enquired Brother Xavier. "There was nothing we could do at the end, was there?"

"No," said the Abbot, reaching for his scorecard. "I meant, I'm sorry I made only four tricks. After you had doubled."

In the other room Brother Paulo and Brother Lucius were facing the stronger of the Italian pairs.

E–W game, dealer East

♠ 10 8 6 4 3
♡ 7 5 2
◇ 10 7
♣ K 8 3

♠ A Q 5
♡ 4
◇ Q 9 8 6 5 2
♣ 9 7 6

♠ K J 9 7 2
♡ 10 8 3
◇ A 4
♣ A 10 4

♠ None
♡ A K Q J 9 6
◇ K J 3
♣ Q J 5 2

South	West	North	East
Bro.	Bro.	Bro.	Bro.
Giacomo	Lucius	Mario	Paulo
			1 ♠
Dble	3 ♠	No	No
4 ♡	End		

Against four hearts Brother Lucius led the ace of spades, ruffed by declarer. Brother Giacomo took one round of trumps and then led the queen of clubs, hoping to establish an entry to dummy for a diamond finesse. Brother Paulo ducked the queen of clubs and ducked again when the jack followed.

Declarer drew a second round of trumps and led a club to the king and ace. East continued the forcing game with another spade. Declarer ruffed, drew the last trump and cashed the thirteenth club. These cards remained:

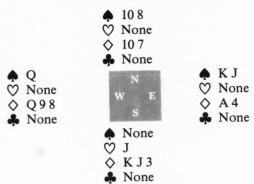

Placing East, the opener, with the ace of diamonds, Brother Giacomo exited with the diamond king. Brother Paulo won the trick and led a spade to force declarer's last trump. West took the next trick with the queen of diamonds but had only a diamond to lead back. Declarer's jack of diamonds provided the game-going trick.

"Yes, you play as sharp as ever," said Brother Paulo, smiling at his old comrade. "Still, there should be no swing on the board. We are lucky to have the Abbot sitting South in the other room."

Exchanging an amused glance with his partner, Brother Lucius reached for the next board. As it happened, West led a diamond at the other table, so the Abbot was not put to the test.

At half-time the Italian monks led by 28 IMPs, much to the annoyance of the Abbot, who had expected them to be tired from their long journey. This hand occurred late in the second half.

N–S game, dealer South

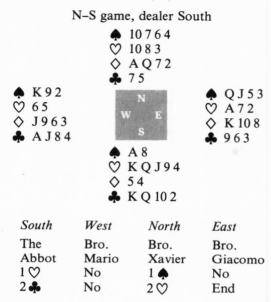

```
                ♠ 10 7 6 4
                ♡ 10 8 3
                ◇ A Q 7 2
                ♣ 7 5
 ♠ K 9 2                        ♠ Q J 5 3
 ♡ 6 5            N             ♡ A 7 2
 ◇ J 9 6 3    W     E           ◇ K 10 8
 ♣ A J 8 4       S              ♣ 9 6 3
                ♠ A 8
                ♡ K Q J 9 4
                ◇ 5 4
                ♣ K Q 10 2
```

South	West	North	East
The	Bro.	Bro.	Bro.
Abbot	Mario	Xavier	Giacomo
1 ♡	No	1 ♠	No
2 ♣	No	2 ♡	End

Mindful of the large deficit, the Abbot considered advancing over two hearts. Eventually he resisted the temptation and West led the three of diamonds.

The Abbot regretted his decision when dummy appeared. The lead made it likely that the diamond finesse was onside; a bit of luck in the club suit and a vulnerable game was there for the taking. Unfortunately there seemed no way he could blame his partner for having stopped short. "Play the queen," he said.

East won with the king and returned a low trump. The Abbot took the trick in dummy and led a club to the queen and ace. The defenders now played two more rounds of trumps. After a losing finesse of the ten of clubs, the Abbot found himself losing three clubs and one trick in each of the other suits. His contract of two hearts was one down.

"Oh, bad luck, Abbot,' exclaimed Brother Xavier. "If you happen to win the first trick with the ace of diamonds, though, can't you play a club immediately to make sure of your ruff?"

"You have a penchant for stating the obvious," declared the Abbot. "With 28 IMPs to be retrieved, I naturally had to go all out for the overtricks."

"We are always beating it if I lead a trump," observed Brother Mario in the West seat.

"Oh yes, to be sure," replied a smiling Brother Giacomo. "So long, of course, that I hold off my trump ace at trick one!"

San Giovanni had won the match by 42 IMPs and the Abbot summoned a thin smile as he congratulated his opponents. "And now, Padre, in case you lose your way in our ramshackle old buildings, Brother Xavier will show you back to your quarters. You've had a long day."

"But it's only ten before twelve," protested Padre Giotto, consulting his pocket watch. "Plenty enough time for a few rubbers! Now, Brother Giacomo, have you seen anywhere my corkscrew?"

3

The Padre's Invitation

The visit of the Italian monks to St. Titus was drawing to a close. The Italians had performed well in the team-of-four matches but had been largely outmanoeuvred at the rubber bridge table.

"That is only what to expecting, Abbot," explained Padre Giotto as they crossed the quadrangle one misty morning. "We are hard-working community at San Giovanni. Rubber bridge is – how you say – a luxury for us."

The Abbot gave a loud sniff. "One would have to travel quite a distance to find a more industrious community than here at St. Titus," he declared. "That reminds me. Where are Brother Damien and Brother Mark? They should be hard at work this very moment, marking the lines on our new tennis court."

That evening a large gathering was present to kibitz the last team-of-four match of the visit. The Abbot, determined to win by a large margin, was fielding his strongest line-up.

Love all, dealer East

$$\begin{array}{ll}
\spadesuit & 6\ 3 \\
\heartsuit & A\ 10\ 7 \\
\diamondsuit & A\ Q\ 9\ 8\ 6\ 4\ 3 \\
\clubsuit & 4
\end{array}$$

$$\begin{array}{ll}
\spadesuit & 10\ 9\ 5 \\
\heartsuit & 9\ 8 \\
\diamondsuit & 10\ 5\ 2 \\
\clubsuit & A\ K\ 9\ 8\ 2
\end{array}$$

$$\begin{array}{ll}
\spadesuit & A\ Q\ J\ 7 \\
\heartsuit & 6\ 4\ 3 \\
\diamondsuit & K\ J\ 7 \\
\clubsuit & J\ 10\ 6
\end{array}$$

$$\begin{array}{ll}
\spadesuit & K\ 8\ 4\ 2 \\
\heartsuit & K\ Q\ J\ 5\ 2 \\
\diamondsuit & None \\
\clubsuit & Q\ 7\ 5\ 3
\end{array}$$

The Padre's Invitation

South	West	North	East
Bro.	Bro.	Bro.	Padre
Paulo	Angelo	Lucius	Giotto
			1 NT
2 ♣	No	3 ◇	No
3 ♡	No	4 ♡	End

The St. Titus pair reached four hearts via an Aspro sequence, Brother Paulo's two club call showing hearts and another suit. When the hearts were rebid, Brother Lucius raised to game in that denomination.

Brother Angelo led the ace of clubs and switched to the nine of trumps. The only way to make the contract was to establish dummy's diamonds, and this would require three entries to dummy in the trump suit. Brother Paulo therefore won the trump switch with dummy's ace, making a spectacular unblock of the king from hand.

"Always the showman!" observed Padre Giotto, raising a finger in mock castigation. "I hope you will not forgetting to mention this at confessional."

"No, indeed," chuckled Brother Paulo, scribbling a reminder to that effect on his scorecard.

The ace of diamonds was played and a diamond ruffed with the queen. Declarer entered dummy with a low heart to the eight and ten and ruffed another diamond with the jack. Diamonds broke three-three and dummy's seven of trumps provided an entry to the rest of the suit. Declarer scored five tricks in each red suit, making his game exactly.

"Yes, I can kill dummy's suit by continuing with second high club," Brother Angelo pointed out. "Is that working?"

"No, I ruff and lead a spade," replied Brother Paulo. "The Padre wins and leads a trump but I still make five trumps, two ruffs and one winner in each side suit."

"All the same, it would be a better defending," declared Padre Giotto, helping himself to a piece of the barley sugar he had been eating throughout the visit. "It would preventing his flashful unblocking play."

The second set saw the two captains in opposition. It was not long before a slam hand arrived.

E–W game, dealer South

```
                ♠ J 10 9 4
                ♡ 6 5 2
                ◇ 7 5
                ♣ A 7 6 3
   ♠ Q 7 6 3      ┌─────────┐      ♠ None
   ♡ Q J 10 7     │    N    │      ♡ K 9 8 4 3
   ◇ 9 6 3        │  W   E  │      ◇ 10 8 4 2
   ♣ J 4          │    S    │      ♣ Q 10 8 5
                  └─────────┘
                ♠ A K 8 5 2
                ♡ A
                ◇ A K Q J
                ♣ K 9 2
```

South	West	North	East
Padre	The	Bro.	Bro.
Giotto	Abbot	Angelo	Xavier
1 ♣	No	1 ◇	No
2 ♠	No	3 ♠	No
4 ♣	No	5 ♣	No
5 NT	No	6 ♠	End

The Italians, playing a version of Precision, were soon sniffing at the grand. Padre Giotto stopped in six when the response to his 5 NT grand slam try denied any of the three top trump honours.

The Abbot led the queen of hearts; East signalled encouragement with the nine and Padre Giotto won in hand. He saw that if trumps were 2–2 he would make thirteen easy tricks. Wondering if they would be in the grand at the other table, he drew one round of trumps with the ace. East showed out, discarding the eight of hearts. Since East had already encouraged hearts at the first trick, the eight showed an even number of cards remaining in the suit.

Padre Giotto continued with a low trump, won by the Abbot's queen. The Abbot paused to consider his return.

"Would you liking barley sweet?" enquired the Padre. "With these we are making big rip-off of tourists at San Giovanni."

"I thank you, no," replied the Abbot, annoyed at the distraction. "I have already dined."

It was clear to the Abbot, both from the bidding and his partner's discard, that there was no heart trick to be cashed. Indeed, a heart return would assist declarer in achieving a dummy reversal. The Abbot therefore exited with a trump.

Declarer won in dummy and ruffed a heart. He then crossed to the ace of clubs and ruffed dummy's last heart high. There was no entry to dummy to draw West's last trump, so declarer had to hope that four rounds of diamonds would stand up. It was not to be. The Abbot ruffed the fourth round and the contract was one down.

In the other room the monastery pair reached six spades on a similar sequence:

South	West	North	East
Bro.	Bro.	Bro.	Bro.
Lucius	Mario	Paulo	Giacomo
2 ♣	No	2 ♦	No
2 ♠	No	3 ♠	No
4 ♦	No	5 ♣	No
5 NT	No	6 ♠	End

Brother Lucius captured the queen of hearts lead and with no noticeable pause for thought continued with the eight of spades from hand. West won and played back a second round of trumps, won in the dummy. Nothing could now prevent declarer ruffing two hearts in hand with high trumps and eventually entering dummy with the ace of clubs to draw West's last trump.

"Yes, a pretty dummy reversing," acknowledged Brother Giacomo. "I believe Padre Giotto will play the contract in other room. I hope he is wide-awoken."

St. Titus led by a promising 26 IMPs at the interval and the Abbot ordered his troops to press home the attack in the second half. The Italians were soon in another slam.

N–S game, dealer North

```
              ♠ A 6
              ♡ K 8 7
              ◇ A K 7 4
              ♣ K Q J 5
  ♠ 10 9 7 3                    ♠ Q 8 5 4 2
  ♡ J 9 6 3        N            ♡ Q 10 5 2
  ◇ Q 10 9 2    W     E         ◇ J
  ♣ 4              S            ♣ 10 6 3
              ♠ K J
              ♡ A 4
              ◇ 8 6 5 3
              ♣ A 9 8 7 2
```

South	West	North	East
Padre	Bro.	Bro.	Bro.
Giotto	Lucius	Angelo	Paulo
		2 NT	No
3 NT	No	4 NT	No
6 ♣	End		

"You knocked for the 3 NT bid?" queried Brother Lucius, who was on lead.

"Yes, it is showing minor suits," replied Brother Angelo.

". . . and 4 NT?"

"He has good help for both minors," replied the Padre, crunching another piece of barley sugar into submission, "and maximum cards."

Brother Lucius led the ten of spades against six clubs. Declarer won in hand, drew trumps in three rounds and eliminated the major suits. This was the end position, with the lead in dummy:

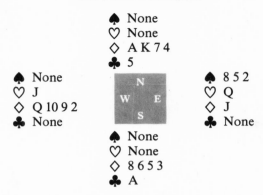

```
              ♠ None
              ♡ None
              ◇ A K 7 4
              ♣ 5
♠ None                        ♠ 8 5 2
♡ J              N            ♡ Q
◇ Q 10 9 2   W     E          ◇ J
♣ None              S         ♣ None
              ♠ None
              ♡ None
              ◇ 8 6 5 3
              ♣ A
```

After some consideration Padre Giotto led a low diamond from the table. The jack appeared from East; Brother Lucius overtook it with the queen and returned the two.

Declarer now had an unpleasant decision to make. Was the jack of diamonds singleton? Or did East have ◇ J 9, ◇ J 10 or ◇ J 10 9, in which case West would doubtless overtake with the queen to give declarer a losing option?

Unwilling to look foolish if the diamonds were 3–2, Padre Giotto eventually called for the ace. East showed out and the slam was one down.

St. Titus had won the match by an unexpected 56 IMPs and the Abbot was in buoyant mood. "Well, Padre," he said. "It seems we have finally settled which is the better team."

"Quite so, quite so," replied Padre Giotto. "Four matches to two in our favour, is it not? You must visit us soon at San Giovanni, Abbot, and maybe make a revenge."

Not likely, thought the Abbot. Who in his right mind would swap the green countryside of Hampshire for the garlic and cockroaches of northern Italy?

"It's a most tempting offer, Padre," he replied. "Unfortunately, with our work schedules being what they are . . . well, it would be nothing short of a miracle if we could spare the time."

4

The Abbot's Unusual Safety Play

Although the Thursday night pairs game at St. Titus was an event of little importance, the Abbot strove his utmost on every hand. His aim was to set the monastery's lesser brethren a target of excellence.

"Not one of our better sessions, Abbot," said Brother Lucius, running a finger down his scorecard. "Half a top over, I make it, and only two rounds to go."

"True, but we haven't played Brother Aelred yet," replied the Abbot, struggling to open a small packet of nuts. "Ah, here he comes!"

N–S game, dealer South

```
              ♠ 8 2
              ♡ A 8 6 5
              ◇ A J 9 4
              ♣ Q 4 2
♠ A J 9 5 3           ♠ 10 7 4
♡ 10 7 3      N      ♡ Q J 9
◇ Q 10 8 5  W   E    ◇ 3
♣ 10          S      ♣ J 9 7 6 5 3
              ♠ K Q 6
              ♡ K 4 2
              ◇ K 7 6 2
              ♣ A K 8
```

South	West	North	East
The	Bro.	Bro.	Bro.
Abbot	Aelred	Lucius	Michael
1 ◇	1 ♠	3 ◇	No
3 NT	End		

Brother Aelred led his fourth best spade against three no-trumps and the Abbot won in hand with the queen. Seeing only eight tricks on top, he surveyed the diamond suit thoughtfully. A straightforward finesse of the jack would be into the dangerous hand.

"Are those cashew nuts, Abbot?" enquired Brother Aelred.

"As a matter of fact they are," replied the Abbot, managing at last to open the wrapping. "My brother brought me a few packs last weekend. He knows they're a weakness of mine."

"That's funny," said Brother Aelred. "I've always liked cashew nuts myself. Not that one sees them very often in our walk of life."

Since he could not afford to let East on lead, the Abbot decided to take a backward finesse in diamonds. He crossed to the ace of diamonds and led the jack from the table. This would pick up the suit without loss if West had started with ◊ 10 x.

"Having none, partner?" said Brother Aelred, somewhat mystified by the Abbot's line of play.

The Abbot ran the trick to West's queen and captured the heart exit in hand. Despite this setback there remained an excellent chance of endplaying West with the fourth round of diamonds. With this in mind the Abbot cashed the other heart honour and three rounds of clubs.

Defending with rare competence, Brother Aelred discarded two spades and retained his third heart. When the diamond exit came, he was able to cross to his partner's queen of hearts. Brother Michael then cashed two master clubs to put the contract one down.

"Well played, Brother Aelred," said Brother Lucius. "That was good defence, holding on to that ten of hearts."

"Well, there was no alternative," said Brother Aelred, reaching learnedly for his scorecard. "I had to protect partner against a possible heart-club squeeze."

The Abbot winced and consoled himself with half a handful of nuts. "It was a trap hand for the expert," he mumbled. "A palooka would have landed the contract with a straightforward finesse in diamonds. Isn't that so, Brother Aelred?"

Brother Lucius unravelled the travelling scoresheet. "H'm. No-one seems to have found your line, Abbot," he said. "Seven 600s and a couple of 630s."

The Abbot shrugged his shoulders and showered the last few nuts directly into his mouth. "The occasional bottom is a cross we experts have to bear," he declared, crunching noisily.

"Maybe the others found the safety play of ace of diamonds followed by the nine, intending to run it," continued Brother Lucius. "When East shows out, declarer can put up the king and lead back towards the jack."

A choking sound came from the South seat.

"Are you all right, Abbot?" enquired Brother Aelred anxiously.

"Of course I hrff . . . hrff . . . am," snapped the Abbot. "This packet of nuts had nothing but hrff . . . salt in the bottom. That's all!"

5

Brother Mark's Alternative Viewing

"I'm going to watch the £1 table for an hour or two," said young Brother Damien, the most aspiring member of the monastery's novitiate. "Are you coming? The Abbot's playing, so there should be some fireworks."

"No, there's a programme on Channel 4 about St. Thomas Aquinas," replied Brother Mark. "I might wander along later."

Brother Damien walked across the top floor of the west wing and into the main card-room, where he drew up a chair behind the monastery's star player, Brother Lucius.

"Plus one," said Brother Lucius, facing his cards. "The spade goes on dummy's long club."

The next hand was soon dealt. These were the cards Brother Damien could see:

Game all, dealer East

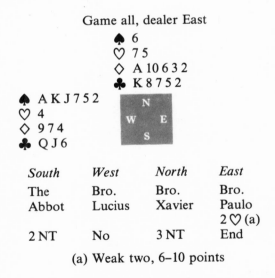

	♠ 6
	♡ 7 5
	◇ A 10 6 3 2
	♣ K 8 7 5 2

♠ A K J 7 5 2
♡ 4
◇ 9 7 4
♣ Q J 6

South	West	North	East
The	Bro.	Bro.	Bro.
Abbot	Lucius	Xavier	Paulo
			2 ♡ (a)
2 NT	No	3 NT	End

(a) Weak two, 6–10 points

Aiming to maintain a link with partner's hand, Brother Lucius led the seven of spades, rather than a top honour. East played the nine, forcing the Abbot's ten. The Abbot now produced king–queen and another diamond, running five tricks in the suit. East discarded the eight–six–two of hearts and Brother Lucius threw one of his spades. He still had to find one more discard from this holding: ♠ A K J 2 ♡ 4 ◇ None ♣ Q J 6.

Brother Damien peered studiously at Lucius's hand, wondering which was the best card to throw. Declarer was almost certainly marked with the ace of clubs, so it had to be assumed that East held the ace of hearts; otherwise declarer would have nine tricks. A club discard might give declarer the whole club suit, thought Brother Damien, so that could be ruled out. And if West threw a heart, he might be thrown in with the third round of clubs to give declarer the spade queen. Yes, the discard had to be another low spade, surely.

Brother Lucius reached for a card and tossed it onto the baize. It was the six of clubs! The Abbot led a heart from dummy, hoping for the best, but East rose with the ace of hearts and the defenders took four spade tricks to put the Abbot one down. This was the whole hand:

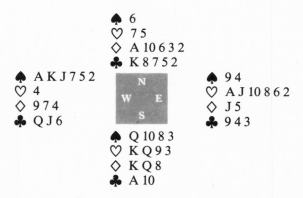

```
              ♠ 6
              ♡ 7 5
              ◇ A 10 6 3 2
              ♣ K 8 7 5 2
 ♠ A K J 7 5 2                    ♠ 9 4
 ♡ 4              N               ♡ A J 10 8 6 2
 ◇ 9 7 4      W       E           ◇ J 5
 ♣ Q J 6          S               ♣ 9 4 3
              ♠ Q 10 8 3
              ♡ K Q 9 3
              ◇ K Q 8
              ♣ A 10
```

A club discard was the only one to beat the contract. If Brother Lucius had thrown a spade, declarer would simply have knocked out the ace of hearts. And if he had thrown his singleton heart, declarer would have been able to endplay him on either the second or third round of clubs, depending on whether he attempted to unblock the honours.

"A somewhat fortunate view on your part, Lucius," grunted the Abbot. "If my distribution had been 3–4–3–3, the only way to beat me would have been to throw your singleton heart on the last diamond."

Brother Lucius nodded his agreement. "That's right, Abbot," he said. "But then Brother Paulo might have helped me by discarding one of his two remaining spades."

The Abbot sniffed dubiously and began to deal the next hand. Brother Damien made a mental note of the hand, intending to study it later. So the choice of discard had been between a heart and a club, had it? How had he made the answer a spade?

The four monks were busy sorting their cards for the next deal.

Game all, dealer South

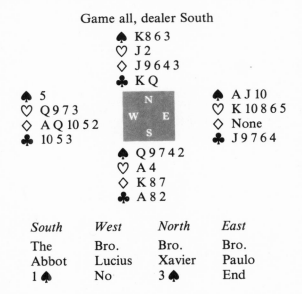

♠ K 8 6 3
♥ J 2
♦ J 9 6 4 3
♣ K Q

♠ 5   ♠ A J 10
♥ Q 9 7 3   ♥ K 10 8 6 5
♦ A Q 10 5 2 ♦ None
♣ 10 5 3   ♣ J 9 7 6 4

♠ Q 9 7 4 2
♥ A 4
♦ K 8 7
♣ A 8 2

South	*West*	*North*	*East*
The	Bro.	Bro.	Bro.
Abbot	Lucius	Xavier	Paulo
1 ♠	No	3 ♠	End

Following his partner's double raise, the Abbot was sorely tempted to bid game. Previous experience of Brother Xavier's double raises eventually swayed him towards passing out three spades.

Brother Lucius led a low heart to the two, ten and ace. The Abbot, assuming a nonchalant air, cashed dummy's two club honours and led a low trump towards his hand.

It seemed natural for Brother Paulo to play low, ensuring two trump tricks, but this would let declarer reach his hand to discard a heart on the ace of clubs.

Brother Damien looked respectfully at the crew-cut bespectacled figure of Brother Paulo, deep in thought. How many years would it be till he could play to the standard of these giants?

Brother Paulo eventually decided to go in with the ace of trumps. His next move was a heart to his partner's queen. There could be only one reason for this heart play, rather than a diamond, and Brother Lucius was quick to underlead the ace of diamonds. East's trump trick returned to the fold, and as the Abbot still had to lose two tricks to the ace and queen of diamonds, he was one down.

"I don't know why you reserve your best efforts for when you're playing against me," declared the Abbot, scribbling the 100 on his scorepad. "We could have done with defences like these in our last Gold Cup match."

Brother Lucius smiled inwardly. He had misdefended a three no-trump contract in a Gold Cup match some five months previously, and the Abbot had referred to it daily ever since.

"And three spades was somewhat excessive on your hand, wasn't it?" the Abbot informed his partner. "Nine losers, I made it."

Brother Mark arrived on the scene and took a seat next to Brother Damien. "Any good hands yet?" he whispered, not wishing to disturb the Abbot's diatribe.

"Hullo," replied Brother Damien. "What happened to St. Thomas Aquinas?"

"Oh, I saw five minutes of it, then Zac and Fabius wanted to switch over to the snooker."

"Ten points? Nearer seven, I make it," continued the Abbot, cutting the cards for Brother Lucius to deal. "The red-suit jacks are virtual waste paper and you can't count five points for king–queen doubleton."

The two postulants exchanged amused glances at this typical performance by the Abbot. Who needed to watch television when the Abbot was at the £1 table?

"Oh dear, oh dear, partner!" came the Abbot's voice as dummy was laid down on the next hand. "Surely you were worth one more try with those good trumps?"

The only problem was . . . no-one had ever found a way of switching him off.

6

The Abbot Absolves

"I have sinned, Father," said Brother Fabius, kneeling uncomfortably on the worn blue hassock.

"The world presents many temptations," replied a gruff voice from within the confessional. "What sins have you committed?"

"Well, on Tuesday afternoon I borrowed Brother Aelred's bicycle without asking him."

"That was discourteous of you. You must apologise to him, and er . . . yes, you can offer to partner him in next Thursday's duplicate."

"But I only borrowed it for half an hour, Abbot," replied Brother Fabius. "Surely that's rather . . ."

"The matter is closed," declared the Abbot blackly. "Have you anything further to confess?"

"Yes, I should like to atone for a hand from last Thursday's pairs. I held ♠ A J 10 6 3 ♡ K 8 4 2 ◇ None ♣ 9 7 6 2 and opened the bidding in the third position with one spade."

"A little underweight, perhaps, but you must have misunderstood my recent ruling. It's only out-and-out psychic bids that have to be reported at the confessional."

"I was merely setting the scene for the play, Abbot. It was there that I let my partner down so badly. This was the hand:

Love all, dealer North

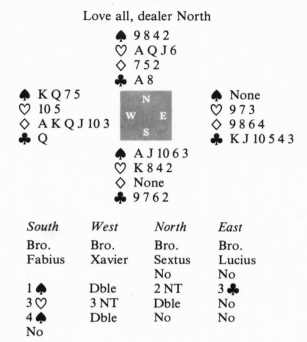

♠ 9 8 4 2
♡ A Q J 6
♢ 7 5 2
♣ A 8

♠ K Q 7 5
♡ 10 5
♢ A K Q J 10 3
♣ Q

♠ None
♡ 9 7 3
♢ 9 8 6 4
♣ K J 10 5 4 3

♠ A J 10 6 3
♡ K 8 4 2
♢ None
♣ 9 7 6 2

South	West	North	East
Bro.	Bro.	Bro.	Bro.
Fabius	Xavier	Sextus	Lucius
		No	No
1 ♠	Dble	2 NT	3 ♣
3 ♡	3 NT	Dble	No
4 ♠	Dble	No	No
No			

"I ruffed the ace of diamonds lead and played the ace of trumps, planning to lose two trumps and a club."

"Yes," replied the Abbot non-committally. "Then what happened?"

"Well, with West holding all four trumps I was in trouble. I had to hope he had four hearts as well and try for a dummy reversal."

"You went one down then, presumably."

"Yes, but Brother Sextus pointed out that I could have made it. If I play the jack of spades at trick two, I can ruff the diamond return and play the ten of spades. Then I can ruff the next diamond with my ace and cross to dummy with a heart to draw trumps."

A pregnant pause came from the confessional.

"That's not right, is it?" said the Abbot eventually. "Instead of forcing you for the third time, West would return a trump. Then you'd be a trick short."

"By St. Christopher, you're right, Abbot!" replied Brother Fabius. "Just wait till I tell Brother Sextus. He's been grumbling about the hand all week."

"Has he indeed?" exclaimed the Abbot. "He was in here not five minutes ago and he never mentioned it."

"Some members of the community are more conscientious than others," remarked Brother Fabius virtuously.

"If no-one else is waiting,. I'll show you a hand from our league match last night," said the Abbot. "I was in four hearts and West led the nine of diamonds."

Game all, dealer South

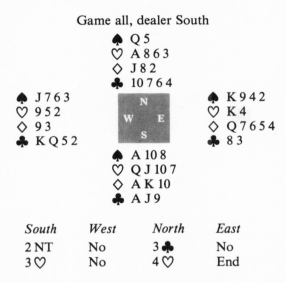

```
              ♠ Q 5
              ♡ A 8 6 3
              ◇ J 8 2
              ♣ 10 7 6 4
♠ J 7 6 3                      ♠ K 9 4 2
♡ 9 5 2          N            ♡ K 4
◇ 9 3         W     E         ◇ Q 7 6 5 4
♣ K Q 5 2        S            ♣ 8 3
              ♠ A 10 8
              ♡ Q J 10 7
              ◇ A K 10
              ♣ A J 9
```

South	West	North	East
2 NT	No	3 ♣	No
3 ♡	No	4 ♡	End

"I won the diamond lead with the ten and ran the queen of hearts to East's king. He returned a diamond, hoping his partner could ruff, so I won in hand and cashed two more rounds of trumps, ending in dummy."

"Er . . . Brother Lucius is waiting to confess, Abbot."

"I can't think why he bothers," grunted the Abbot. "He never admits to anything worthwhile. Anyway, I now played a club to the jack and queen, and West exited with a low spade. Which card do you play from dummy?"

"I've no idea," said Brother Fabius. "It's a complete guess, isn't it?"

"It would be for most players," replied the Abbot, "but I managed to unravel quite a subtle line of reasoning."

"Did you, Abbot? How interesting," said Brother Fabius, shifting his knees on the rock-hard hassock.

"You can place West with the club king, can't you?" continued the Abbot, quite happy to keep Brother Lucius waiting. "Otherwise the spade guess is irrelevant . . ."

"Yes, I see," nodded Brother Fabius.

". . . and if West held both black kings and had to decide which one to underlead at this point, he would surely prefer a club."

"Why's that?" asked Brother Fabius, aware that the Abbot would explain anyway.

"Well, a club would be safe if declarer held ♣ A J alone, or if he misguessed with ♣ A J 8. A spade return, on the other hand, would be all too likely to run into an ace–jack tenace. Indeed, had I not added a point for my three tens, I would be marked with the ace–jack of spades to make up a 20-count."

"Oh, I say, Abbot. How clever!"

"Yes. I played low from dummy and the king came from East. Just as well, because the other club honour did prove to be offside. Send in Lucius, will you?"

Brother Lucius stepped forward and knelt down with a dignified air. "I regret I lost control of myself in the refectory this morning, Abbot," he said. "I let loose a sharp word to Brother Anthony."

"He was sent to try us all," replied the Abbot. "Burnt toast again, was it?"

"No, he spilt some boiling tea in my lap."

"Oh yes," replied the Abbot, not sounding very interested. "I was just showing Fabius that game swing from the match. Presumably the declarer in your room was less able than myself."

"Almost certainly, Abbot," said Brother Lucius. "But on this occasion he had little chance. I was East at the other table and when the trump finesse lost, I returned a club to break up the endplay. Declarer tried playing low, but . . ."

"Enough!" interrupted the Abbot fiercely. "The confessional is hardly the place to seek praise for your exploits at the card table."

The Abbot paused to consider a suitable penance.

"This is a grave offence, Brother Lucius," he declared eventually. "As it happens, I overheard Brother Aelred this morning saying that he had been unable to find a partner for next month's National Pairs qualifier." He paused to let his words sink in. "I'm sure I need explain no further. You may go."

7

An Unforeseen Ending

The venerable St. Titus, founder of the monastery, had not been a bridge player himself. Indeed the game was unknown in 1537, the year of the monastery's foundation. According to Vatican records, though, he had been a leading player of Ryckettes-Boule, a French card game not dissimilar to Bezique. He had in fact been canonised following a hand where his partner had missed an obvious unblock of the queen of Batons. Despite losing over three guineas on the hand, St. Titus had forgiven his partner instantly and insisted on paying his losses in an attempt to console him. The Abbot often spoke of this incident when addressing new members of the Order.

To commemorate the event, the monks held a Gala Pairs once a year to compete for the Beatification Salver. The novel feature on this occasion was to be a draw for partners. As was the custom, the Abbot stood alone on the dais drawing names from a silver urn.

Early on, he drew the combination of himself and Brother Paulo. "Last year," he remarked, "you may remember that Brother Lucius carried this old war-horse to second place. We must see what the Italian Job can do."

Soon after he called: "Pair No. 7. Brother Aelred and . . ." the room hushed ". . . Brother Lucius." The Abbot removed his glasses and looked up. "An opportunity for this pair to build on their experience in the National Pairs," he remarked. There was a burst of laughter from the contestants, who all knew that Brother Lucius and Brother Aelred had finished 26th in a 13-table qualifier.

The draw was soon over and the room was filled with the sound of bidding systems being discussed. The Abbot raised his hand for silence. "One thing more," he announced. "This year I thought we might hold a 50p sweepstake on the event."

Brother Lucius shook his head piously. "Surely the honour of winning the Beatification Salver is ample recompense to the successful pair," he said. There was a murmur of assent from other monks not enchanted by the draw.

"So be it," declared the Abbot, as if he had little interest in the affair. The event, an extended 32-board session, was soon under way. Brother Paulo and the Abbot began strongly. In the fifth round they faced Brother Damien who was partnered, rather incongruously, by the aged Brother Zac.

At the Monastery of St. Titus

Love all, dealer West

```
              ♠ 3
              ♡ K 8 2
              ◇ K Q 4
              ♣ A Q 10 9 6 2
♠ A Q 9 7 5 2      N        ♠ K 10
♡ 9 5 4                      ♡ Q J 7 3
◇ J 7          W      E      ◇ 10 9 6 3
♣ 7 4              S         ♣ K 5 3
              ♠ J 8 6 4
              ♡ A 10 6
              ◇ A 8 5 2
              ♣ J 8
```

South	West	North	East
The	Bro.	Bro.	Bro.
Abbot	Zac	Paulo	Damien
	2 ♠	3 ♣	No
3 NT	No	No	No

"My call, is it?" said Brother Zac, glancing down at his convention card. "Two spades."

"Acol two, presumably?" asked Brother Paulo.

"No, we all prefer weak twos in the novitiate," replied Brother Damien earnestly. "Brother Zac kindly agreed to play them on this occasion."

Brother Paulo overcalled three clubs and the Abbot closed the auction with a call of 3 NT.

The seven of spades was led and Brother Damien, sitting East, contributed the ten. Somewhat mystified at this stroke of good fortune, the Abbot took the trick with his jack and immediately ran the jack of clubs. When Brother Damien won and returned the king of spades, West overtook and cashed the rest of the spade suit to put the contract two down.

The Abbot shrugged his shoulders and turned to address Brother Damien. "You should have played your king on the first trick," he informed him. "Even a beginner should know that, surely? You gave me an unnecessary spade trick."

"Yes, I see, Abbot. But wouldn't the spade suit have been blocked then?"

"Er . . . as it happens, but . . ."

"I'm probably quite wrong," continued Brother Damien, "but the Rule of 11 put you with two cards higher than the seven, and it seemed to me that the only chance was to find you with J 8 x x or Q 8 x x and to tempt you to win the first trick."

"Yes, could you not duck the first trick, Abbot?" enquired Brother Paulo. "The 11-rule places East with one more card higher than the seven, is it not? If it's the nine, West must have the A K Q and therefore not the club king, so you're down anyhow. If it's any higher card, it will be blocking the suit when you duck the first trick."

"A superficial analysis," declared the Abbot with a wave of the hand. "Have you filled in the score yet?"

Brother Paulo opened the scoresheet and entered the 100 in a virgin East–West column. "Yes, even five clubs is making," he observed. "A red-suit squeeze on East, I think."

A round or two later, the Abbot arrived at Brother Lucius's table.

E–W game, dealer South

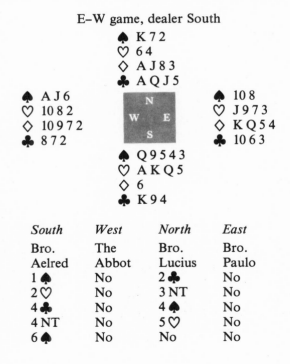

```
              ♠ K 7 2
              ♡ 6 4
              ◇ A J 8 3
              ♣ A Q J 5
♠ A J 6                        ♠ 10 8
♡ 10 8 2          N           ♡ J 9 7 3
◇ 10 9 7 2    W     E         ◇ K Q 5 4
♣ 8 7 2          S            ♣ 10 6 3
              ♠ Q 9 5 4 3
              ♡ A K Q 5
              ◇ 6
              ♣ K 9 4
```

South	West	North	East
Bro.	The	Bro.	Bro.
Aelred	Abbot	Lucius	Paulo
1 ♠	No	2 ♣	No
2 ♡	No	3 NT	No
4 ♣	No	4 ♠	No
4 NT	No	5 ♡	No
6 ♠	No	No	No

[37]

Brother Lucius's efforts to restrain the bidding were to no avail. Brother Aelred sailed into the spade slam and the Abbot led the ten of diamonds.

"Only three trumps?" queried Brother Aelred when the dummy appeared. "I thought you'd have four. I never rebid my spades, did I?"

"I'm sorry. The point escaped me," replied Brother Lucius. "Try your best, anyhow."

Brother Aelred won the lead with dummy's ace and ruffed a diamond in hand. Not liking to test the frail holding in the trump suit, he crossed twice in clubs to ruff two more diamonds. Three rounds of hearts were cashed, dummy discarding a club, and this end position was reached:

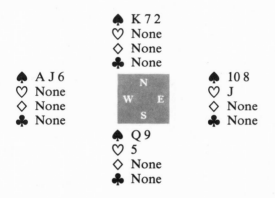

```
               ♠ K 7 2
               ♡ None
               ◇ None
               ♣ None
  ♠ A J 6         N          ♠ 10 8
  ♡ None      W       E      ♡ J
  ◇ None          S          ◇ None
  ♣ None                     ♣ None
               ♠ Q 9
               ♡ 5
               ◇ None
               ♣ None
```

Brother Aelred led the 5 of hearts and the Abbot ruffed with the jack – his only chance. Dummy overruffed and a low trump was led, East following small.

Brother Aelred screwed up his eyes in thought. What should he play from hand, the nine or the queen? Suddenly inspiration came to him. Of course! East had turned up already with K Q of diamonds and the jack of hearts. With the ace of trumps as well, and playing against me, he would surely have doubled the slam! Smiling confidently to himself, he finessed the nine and made the contract.

The Abbot gazed blankly in front of him. "Now I've seen everything," he declared. "Quite unjustified bidding followed by an even worse line of play, and then a miraculous lie of the cards lets the contract home."

Brother Lucius unravelled the scoresheet with a seeming lack of concern. "Yes, it's the only 980 so far," he reported.

"Why in heaven's name didn't you simply play for one of us to have ace doubleton of trumps?" continued the Abbot.

"Well, I thought about it" replied Brother Aelred carefully. "But it didn't seem very good odds."

"Not very good odds?" exclaimed the Abbot. "What do you think the odds are of finding clubs 3-3, diamonds 4-4, hearts 3-4 and East holding 10 8 or J 8 doubleton of spades?"

Brother Lucius proffered the scoresheet for the Abbot's perusal but the Abbot waved it aside. "I put dummy play like that on a par with frivolous psyching," he declared severely. "Just because you have no chance of winning yourself, Brother Aelred, that's no excuse for upsetting the natural order of those who are in contention."

"But Brother Lucius made us almost three tops above average at the end of the last round," said Brother Aelred. "That's why I tried so hard on the slam."

The Abbot blinked in disbelief, then managed a brief chuckle. "What bad luck for you, Lucius," he said. "You shouldn't have vetoed my innocent suggestion of a sweepstake."

8

The Abbot's Matchwinning Board

Without warning it started to rain. The Abbot reached forward to switch on the windscreen wipers. "What number are we looking for?" he said.

"Number 35, I think," replied Brother Lucius, peering out of a side window. "Can you slow down a bit, Abbot? Ah, yes. 27 . . . 29 . . . you can park over there, behind the green Volvo."

"I'm quite capable of parking without assistance," grunted the Abbot, ignoring the large space behind the Volvo and trying to manoeuvre into a much smaller space the other side of it.

The monastery team were soon seated in the warmth of Mrs. Port-Binding's bungalow, playing in a county knockout match.

Love all, dealer South

♠ J 10 8 2
♡ Q 10 4
◇ J 8 5 3
♣ 10 4

♠ A Q
♡ K 9 2
◇ 9 4
♣ A K Q J 9 3

♠ 4
♡ J 8 6 3
◇ 10 7 6 2
♣ 8 6 5 2

♠ K 9 7 6 5 3
♡ A 7 5
◇ A K Q
♣ 7

South	West	North	East
Bro.	Mrs.	The	Mrs.
Lucius	P–B	Abbot	Stott
1 ♠	Dble	2 ♠	No
4 ♠	Dble	End	

Mrs. Port-Binding led the ace of clubs against four spades doubled, and after a brief inspection of the dummy continued with the king.

Brother Lucius ruffed in hand and soon spotted a reasonable chance of making the contract.

His first move was to cash his three diamond winners. On the third round he was pleased to see Mrs. Port-Binding shifting uneasily in her seat. Eventually she decided to discard a club. Brother Lucius continued with the king of trumps from hand and Mrs. Port-Binding found she was endplayed. After cashing a second round of trumps she exited with a low heart, hoping for the best. Brother Lucius put up the queen and discarded his other heart loser on the jack of diamonds, claiming the contract.

"Well, no-one can say I didn't have my double," declared Mrs. Port-Binding as she returned her cards to the wallet. "I had 19 points, partner!"

"I wonder if there's any possible defence," said Brother Lucius. "Suppose . . . yes, suppose you switch to a diamond at trick 2. Then you have a safe exit in clubs when I put you in."

The elderly Mrs. Stott glared across the table. "I did discourage clubs, partner," she observed. "Didn't you see my 2?"

Brother Lucius smiled. "Perhaps the 6, a length signal, would have been even more helpful," he suggested.

Welcoming this support from an unexpected quarter, Mrs. Port-Binding nodded her head. "Give me the six of clubs, Eleanor, and a diamond switch stands out a mile."

Even a heart switch would beat it, thought Brother Lucius as he wrote down the score. The board was soon replayed in the other room. This was the auction:

South	West	North	East
Mr.	Bro.	Mrs.	Bro.
Carver	Xavier	Carver	Paulo
1 ♠	3 NT	No	No
No			

Brother Xavier opted for the straightforward call of 3NT and no further bidding resulted. He won the jack of spades lead with the queen and crossed to dummy on the third round of clubs to lead a heart. When South played low, Brother Xavier rose successfully with the king and claimed nine tricks.

"Rather lucky there, partner," he observed. "The diamonds were wide open all the time."

Mr. Carver, a retired tax inspector, offered his ◇ A K Q for Brother Xavier's inspection. "I would hardly play low on the heart if we had a chance of four diamond tricks," he said. "I could count you for eight tricks in the black suits, after all."

"Yes, of course," apologised Brother Xavier. "We were extremely fortunate."

"We can beat it at double dummy, I fancy," continued Mr. Carver, tapping out the contents of his pipe. "Marguerite leads a diamond. I cash my three honours and exit safely with a club."

"True," agreed Brother Paulo. "It is interesting also on a club lead, I think. Declarer takes a second round of clubs and exits in diamonds. You must play one major suit for him, and he can cross in clubs to lead the other major."

With the help of this board the monastery team led by 18 IMPs at half-time.

"Just 18?" queried the Abbot. "I must say I was hoping for more than that with our card."

"Really?" said Brother Paulo. "Which boards were you thinking of, Abbot?"

"Well, the Port-Binding woman made an absolute pig's-ear of 3 NT on board . . ."

"Is the tea all right for you?" asked Mrs. Port-Binding, poking her head round the door. "Not too strong, is it?"

The match soon resumed. A hand late in the last set saw Brother Lucius in a tight diamond slam.

N–S game, dealer North

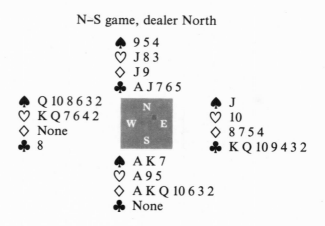

```
              ♠ 9 5 4
              ♡ J 8 3
              ◇ J 9
              ♣ A J 7 6 5
♠ Q 10 8 6 3 2                    ♠ J
♡ K Q 7 6 4 2         N           ♡ 10
◇ None          W         E       ◇ 8 7 5 4
♣ 8                   S           ♣ K Q 10 9 4 3 2
              ♠ A K 7
              ♡ A 9 5
              ◇ A K Q 10 6 3 2
              ♣ None
```

South	West	North	East
Bro.	Mrs.	The	Mrs.
Lucius	P-B	Abbot	Stott
		No	3 ♣
6 ◇	No	No	No

The ♣ 8 was led against six diamonds and Brother Lucius surveyed the disappointing dummy. Prospects were extremely poor. Indeed his best chance seemed to be to find East with a singleton king or queen in hearts.

Brother Lucius looked again at the dummy's club pips. They were just good enough to establish a tenace against East. Yes. If East's distribution was 1–2–3–7 with a doubleton heart honour, it should be possible to create a club tenace and endplay East on the second round of hearts.

Following this plan, Brother Lucius covered ♣ 8 with the jack and ruffed East's queen. He cashed ♡ A, just in case East held a singleton king or queen, and continued with ◇ 6 to dummy's nine, raising an eyebrow when West showed out. So East held four trumps! Since she hadn't made a Lightner double it was heavy odds that she had a 1–1–4–7 distribution.

Brother Lucius led ♣ 7 from dummy, covered by the nine and ruffed with the ace. He now overtook ◇ 10 with the jack and led ♣ 6. Once again East had to cover, or declarer would remain in dummy and cash the club ace. Declarer ruffed high again and cashed the queen of trumps and the spade ace. This was the end position:

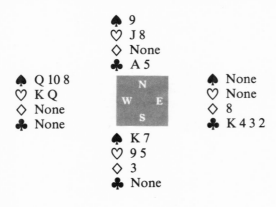

Brother Lucius led his last trump, throwing a heart from dummy, and East had to win and lead into the club tenace. This restored the trick given up in trumps, and the second club trick squeezed West in the majors for a twelfth.

"Yes, well done, partner," said the Abbot. "But isn't it simpler to discard a spade on the ace of clubs and run the diamonds? West must come down to ♠ Q 10 and ♡ K Q 7, and then you have him."

The final comparison was soon in progress and not going too well for the monastery team.

"+ 120," said the Abbot.

"Oh dear, you weren't doubled?" said Brother Xavier. "That's strange. I had an excellent 14-count. − 380. That's er . . . 6 IMPs away."

"+ 110," continued the Abbot. "That must be good, surely? They had two chances to get me down."

"− 100," said Brother Xavier. "They pushed us up to three clubs, I'm afraid, and the trumps broke 4–1."

"Are you allergic to plus scores?" snapped the Abbot. "Anyway, here's our matchwinner. + 1370! We made six diamonds."

"Yes, flat board," replied Brother Xavier.

"I don't believe it!" exclaimed the Abbot. "Those old dodderers brought home six diamonds?"

"No problem, was there?" said Brother Xavier. "She won the king of hearts in hand, drew trumps and . . ."

"Well, what a surprise!" said Mrs. Port-Binding, leading her victorious team into the room. "We never expected to win this one, I must say. And what a triumph for Marguerite Carver, making that difficult diamond slam. She hasn't been playing very long, you know. Now, can I offer you a drink before you go?"

"Ah, the cup that cheers," said the aged Mrs. Stott, seating herself in anticipation.

"I thank you, no," said the Abbot, who had tasted Mrs. Port-Binding's home-made potions before. "Come on, you three! My car will need a push-start in this wet weather."

9

Brother Zac Gives a Ruling

The annual pairs championship for the St. Titus salver was traditionally held in the first week after Candlemas. On this occasion Brother Lucius, the monastery accountant, was unable to participate. A visit from H.M. Tax Inspectors was impending and Brother Lucius had been working round the clock in preparation.

Not one to miss an opportunity, the Abbot had decided to test Brother Xavier at a higher level. Early in the evening they faced Brother Paulo, who was partnered by the rapidly improving Brother Damien.

Game all, dealer West

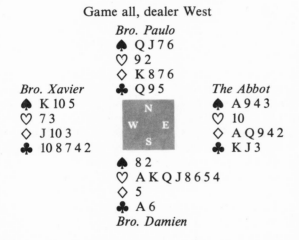

Bro. Paulo
♠ Q J 7 6
♡ 9 2
◇ K 8 7 6
♣ Q 9 5

Bro. Xavier
♠ K 10 5
♡ 7 3
◇ J 10 3
♣ 10 8 7 4 2

The Abbot
♠ A 9 4 3
♡ 10
◇ A Q 9 4 2
♣ K J 3

♠ 8 2
♡ A K Q J 8 6 5 4
◇ 5
♣ A 6
Bro. Damien

The Abbot, sitting East, opened one diamond, Brother Damien overcalled four hearts, and two passes followed.

"Have you passed, Abbot?" enquired Brother Xavier.

"Not that I'm aware of," replied the Abbot. "One spade."

There was an embarrassed silence.

"Er . . . that's not sufficient, Abbot," said young Brother Damien. "I bid four hearts."

"*Four* hearts?" said the Abbot, looking up sharply. "I heard one heart. Why can't you speak up?"

"You are allowed to make the bid good, Abbot," pointed out Brother Paulo, with one eye on his ♠ Q J x x.

"No, no, of course not," replied the Abbot. "Your lead, partner. Come on, we've wasted enough time as it is."

Brother Damien summoned up his courage. "Shouldn't we call the director, Abbot?" he said.

His patience wearing thin, the Abbot summoned the elderly Brother Zac, who was serving a week's penance as director.

"Our young friend here bid most indistinctly," the Abbot informed Brother Zac, "as a result of which I made an insufficient bid. I am, of course, allowed to substitute a pass."

Brother Zac flicked through his rule book, eventually finding the appropriate section. "Yes, that seems to be in order," he announced.

"Let's go, then," said the Abbot, beckoning Brother Xavier to make the opening lead.

"Of course, there may be a lead penalty," continued Brother Zac. "What's this footnote here? It refers to page 26. Let me look."

The Abbot could take no more. He sat back in his chair and pretended to doze off.

"Here we are. Call in Rotation after an Illegal Call. That's not what we want, is it? Perhaps it was *Law* 26, not page 26 . . ."

Brother Zac licked his finger and turned the pages once more. "Ah yes, that's more like it. Unauthorised Information Given by Change of Call. Now, the denomination was a suit, wasn't it? Yes, here we are. Well, it looks to me as though declarer may either require or forbid the lead of the suit illegally called. Spades, wasn't it? Hold on, there's another footnote. No, it makes no difference. It looks to me, then, that Brother Damien may either require or forbid a spade lead." Brother Zac beamed at everyone, in the assurance of a difficult job well done.

Brother Damien decided to bar a spade lead and Brother Xavier selected the 3 of hearts. The 2 was played from dummy and there was a short interval while the Abbot performed the motions of a man awaking from a long sleep. Brother Damien won the Abbot's ten with the ace and led a spade towards dummy. Brother Xavier stepped in smartly with the king and switched to the jack of diamonds. Declarer covered with dummy's king and the contract was now secure. He could establish a spade trick for a club discard and reach it with dummy's 9 of trumps.

"What a feeble switch, partner!" declared the Abbot. "Surely it's obvious we need a club trick to beat the contract."

"I was hoping for two diamond tricks," replied Brother Xavier.

The Abbot reached impatiently for the next board. "With only four diamonds, I would have reopened with a double," he said. "Not one spade."

Brother Paulo smiled at his young partner. "It's rather surprising, but if you are demanding a spade lead the contract is quite cold."

"No, it's not. I can lead the king of spades and switch to a club," said Brother Xavier, looking pleased with himself. "Yes, I'm sure I would have found that defence, Abbot."

"The rules are not allowing you to switch while you hold the lead," Brother Paulo informed him.

"No, you're wrong there," said Brother Zac, who had stayed to watch the hand. "This situation came up in the Joseph of Arimathea Swiss Teams event. The rule not to switch applies only when declarer has prohibited the lead of a . . ."

"Thank you for your help, Brother Zac," interrupted the Abbot. "If we need any further assistance, we'll call you. Come on, Brother Damien. It's your call on the next board."

East–West game, dealer South

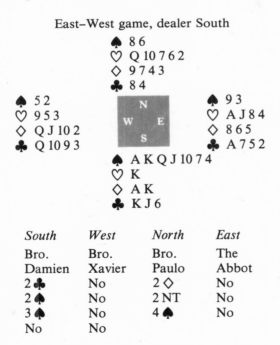

```
                  ♠ 8 6
                  ♡ Q 10 7 6 2
                  ◇ 9 7 4 3
                  ♣ 8 4
  ♠ 5 2                           ♠ 9 3
  ♡ 9 5 3              N          ♡ A J 8 4
  ◇ Q J 10 2       W     E        ◇ 8 6 5
  ♣ Q 10 9 3           S          ♣ A 7 5 2
                  ♠ A K Q J 10 7 4
                  ♡ K
                  ◇ A K
                  ♣ K J 6
```

South	West	North	East
Bro.	Bro.	Bro.	The
Damien	Xavier	Paulo	Abbot
2♣	No	2◇	No
2♠	No	2 NT	No
3♠	No	4♠	No
No	No		

Brother Xavier led the queen of diamonds and Brother Damien won in hand. He now played the king of hearts. The Abbot took the trick and returned another diamond.

Needing a club ruff, Brother Damien now had to guess which club honour to lead. If West had to win the club, he would not be able to play a trump without giving declarer an entry to dummy and the established queen of hearts.

Since East had already shown up with one ace, Brother Damien misguessed the position, leading the king of clubs from hand. The Abbot won and returned the 3 of spades. After some thought, Brother Damien played with the odds by running this to dummy's 8. To win in hand would gain only if West held a singleton 9, or if East's 3 was a singleton and he had the club queen.

When this manoeuvre proved successful, Brother Damien discarded a club on the queen of hearts and claimed the contract.

"I did my best," said the Abbot wearily. "If my partner leads a trump, of course, it's a different matter."

"But doesn't a trump lead give him an entry to dummy, Abbot?" said Brother Xavier.

"Do you think an old fox like me would part with the 9?" countered the Abbot. "Of course not. I would leave him in dummy at trick one, before the heart is established."

"But then he can lead a club . . ."

"Yes, but there's no reason why he shouldn't try the jack," persisted the Abbot. "You win with the queen and return another trump. Declarer will doubtless run the trump suit, but there's no endplay so long as I hold on to my three small diamonds."

"You are seeming in very good form tonight, Abbot," said Brother Paulo. "You must be a strong favourite to win the salver."

The Abbot shook his head at this suggestion and bent forward to whisper in Brother Paulo's ear. "Lester Piggott never won the Derby on a carthorse," he said.

10

Brother Aelred's Condolences

Brother Zac's finger moved slowly along the illuminated manuscript. "... tibi debitum obsequium praestare valeamus," he muttered. "Hm ... we may be worthy ... to stand before ..."

"Hey, have you heard the news?" said Brother Fabius, entering the library suddenly. "Brother Aelred is 17 IMPs up on the Abbot with only eight boards left!"

"We must lend support to our superior," replied Brother Zac, hastily pushing the manuscript to one side. "Where are they playing? In the main card room?"

During the month of August the monks held a league within the monastery to sharpen their game for the Gold Cup. Each team was handicapped according to its abilities and, tonight, news was spreading round the monastery that the Abbot (Scratch) was making hard work of his match against Brother Aelred (+40 IMPs). Only four boards remained when this hand was dealt:

Game all, dealer North

♠ Q
♥ A J 5
♦ A 9 2
♣ A K Q 8 6 5

♠ K 7 5
♥ 9 4
♦ K 8
♣ J 10 9 7 3 2

♠ A J 9 6 4 2
♥ 10 8 2
♦ J 6 3
♣ 4

♠ 10 8 3
♥ K Q 7 6 3
♦ Q 10 7 5 4
♣ None

South	West	North	East
The	Bro.	Bro.	Bro.
Abbot	Aelred	Lucius	Michael
		1 ♣	1 ♠
2 ♡	2 ♠	3 ♠	No
4 ◇	No	6 ♡	No
No	No		

Respecting his partner's overcall, Brother Aelred led a spade against six hearts. East won and continued with another spade, ruffed in dummy.

As far as the Abbot could see, there were two plausible lines of play. He could cash dummy's two top trumps, return to hand with a club ruff and draw trumps. This would succeed if clubs were 4–3 or West held the singleton king of diamonds. Alternatively he could cash the ace of hearts, ruff a club in hand, ruff a spade with the jack of hearts, ruff another club and attempt to draw trumps in two more rounds. This line would need a 3–2 trump break and the clubs no worse than 5–2.

"What's the contract?" asked a breathless Brother Zac, joining the two dozen or so kibitzers gathered round the table.

"Six hearts," replied Brother Sextus. "This hand could decide the match; they didn't pick up much on the previous four boards."

"Would you be quiet," said the Abbot, looking round and noticing for the first time the large number of onlookers. Rather odd, he thought. Hardly anyone had watched last year, when they beat Brother Aelred's team by 102 IMPs.

Now, which was the better line? Ruffing a second spade and ruffing clubs twice would need trumps 3–2 (68%) and clubs no worse then 5–2 (93%), combined odds of about 63%. The other line (cashing two trumps and ruffing clubs once) would need trumps 4–1 or better (96%) and either a 4–3 club break (62%) or the king of diamonds to . . .

"What contract is he in?" asked the 82 year-old Brother Jake, who had insisted on being wheeled out of the infirmary to witness the occasion.

"Ssh!" replied Brother Zac in a stage whisper. "He's in six hearts and can't decide how to play it."

All figures driven from his mind, the Abbot abandoned his calculations. The two lines were doubtless very close, anyhow. He cashed the ace and jack of hearts, ruffed a club and drew the last trump. When the clubs failed to break, he guessed the diamonds correctly but was still one down.

"Isn't it better to ruff another spade?" queried Brother Lucius.

"My line was superior by 0.47%," replied the Abbot. "It's hardly relevant though. Clubs were 6–1, so both lines fail. Pass the next board, will you?"

"Are you sure, Abbot? A second spade ruff gives you eleven tricks and then West is squeezed in the minors for a twelfth. East holds three trumps, so he can't damage you by ruffing the second club."

The Abbot and Brother Lucius gathered a few points on the remaining hands, mostly part scores, and it seemed that the result would indeed depend on the slam hand. The Abbot looked up at the assembly of monks who stood with downcast eyes, waiting for the match to be scored. "This isn't a chimpanzees' tea party," he declared. "Have you no duties to perform?"

The Abbot's other pair soon returned. "We've done fairly well," said Brother Xavier. "They made one slam, but apart from that we . . ."

"They made six hearts on board 21?" gasped the Abbot. "I don't believe it."

"Six hearts? No, they were in six diamonds, Abbot" said Brother Xavier. "Hearts were never mentioned. The lead was a . . ."

"Six diamonds?" demanded the Abbot. "Are we talking about the same board? There's a spade loser and at least one trump loser, surely?"

"Well, he lost a spade all right, but no trump tricks," said Brother Xavier. "The jack of clubs was led, declarer discarding a spade from hand. He continued with a second high club, which I ruffed and he overruffed."

"Yes, then what?"

"He returned to dummy with a heart and led another high club. I ruffed, he overruffed again and led the queen of diamonds, pinning my jack and allowing him to pick up the trump suit without loss. He knew I couldn't have the king of diamonds, of course, or I would have ruffed high earlier and cashed a spade. Anyhow, there was still a trump left in dummy to take an eventual spade ruff, so twelve tricks were there."

Brother Lucius had been listening to the tale with a weary expression. "Why did you ruff the second time?" he said. "Only one ruff is necessary. If you discard on the third club, declarer must lose a spade and a trump."

When scores were compared, the Abbot's worst suspicions were confirmed. Brother Aelred had triumphed by 5 IMPs.

"Well, you played a good game, Abbot. You had us worried near the end," said Brother Aelred, acting as host in the monastery buttery. "It was most unlucky to lose the match just by playing that slam in the wrong suit, but these things can happen to the best of teams, believe me. Now, winning captain's round, I insist. How about a ginger beer shandy?"

11

Brother Xavier's Indiscretion

"Yes, I make the rubber 15 points," said the Abbot, shaking his head unhappily. "Lead back the queen of diamonds, partner, and we live to fight another day." Reluctantly he reached into an old leather wallet and extracted three £5 notes. "Table up!" he said.

The tall figure of Brother Anthony, member of the silent Eustacian order, approached the table.

"Are you coming in?" enquired the Abbot stonily.

Brother Anthony confirmed this intention with a slight nod of the head and the players cut the pack to see who should sit out. The Abbot took no part in this procedure. One of his long-established privileges was that he could sit at the £1 table as long as he wished.

Love all, dealer North

```
                    ♠ A K 4
                    ♡ K Q 9
                    ◇ K 9 7 6
                    ♣ A K Q
   ♠ 10 9 8 3          N            ♠ 7 6 2
   ♡ A 4          W        E        ♡ J 7 3
   ◇ J 8 5 2                        ◇ 10 4 3
   ♣ 10 7 2            S            ♣ 8 6 5 3
                    ♠ Q J 5
                    ♡ 10 8 6 5 2
                    ◇ A Q
                    ♣ J 9 4
```

South	West	North	East
Bro.	Bro.	The	Bro.
Sextus	Anthony	Abbot	Xavier
		2 ♣	No
2 NT	No	3 NT	No
6 NT	No	No	No

The Abbot's satisfaction at avoiding Brother Anthony in the draw for partners was enhanced by the sight of his first hand. A brief auction put Brother Sextus in 6 NT and the ten of spades was led. Since he needed to attack hearts from his own hand, Brother Sextus ran the spade lead to his queen. A heart to the king held the next trick and he returned to hand with the ace of diamonds. Now, he thought, which heart should he play from dummy on the next trick? Was Brother Xavier being clever, holding off the ace? Still undecided, Brother Sextus led a low heart from hand. The ace appeared on his left and he gave a satisfied sigh. Then suddenly he realised that the heart suit would be blocked if he played low from dummy. A diamond switch from West would cut him off from the long hearts.

Brother Sextus surveyed dummy's cards unhappily. If East held ♡ J x an unblock of the heart queen would succeed. But if West held ♡ A x x, he might well have ducked twice to put declarer to a guess.

Eventually Brother Sextus decided to play low from dummy, hoping West would misdefend. Brother Anthony rarely erred in defence, though. Since his vow of silence precluded him from taking any part in the bidding and so becoming the declarer, defence was the strongest part of his game. With no change of expression he played back a second round of diamonds. No miracle occurred when the last few tricks were played out, so declarer was one down.

"A sad waste of my 24-count," declared the Abbot. "You had five hearts, didn't you? Why on earth didn't you mention them? Six hearts was frigid."

"That's true," said Brother Xavier, well pleased to take a plus score on the hand. "But wasn't there a way to make 6 NT?" He turned towards Brother Sextus. "Suppose you win the spade lead in dummy, not in hand. Then you can cross twice in diamonds to lead towards the heart honours. The hearts become blocked, as before, but West can't remove your spade entry. You make twelve tricks easily."

"I didn't want to mention that," said the Abbot virtuously. "I don't know. There seems to be a blight on my partners this afternoon."

The rubber ended all square, a small triumph for Brother Xavier in the circumstances. The Abbot once again escaped Brother Anthony in the cut, and the next rubber had reached game all when the following hand was dealt.

Game all, dealer West

Bro. Anthony
♠ K J 10 7
♡ 3
♢ K 9 7 6 5
♣ 8 5 4

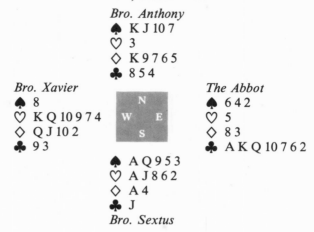

Bro. Xavier
♠ 8
♡ K Q 10 9 7 4
♢ Q J 10 2
♣ 9 3

The Abbot
♠ 6 4 2
♡ 5
♢ 8 3
♣ A K Q 10 7 6 2

Bro. Sextus
♠ A Q 9 5 3
♡ A J 8 6 2
♢ A 4
♣ J

West and North passed, leaving the Abbot with an interesting tactical situation. It seemed likely that North–South had the values for game somewhere, so what was the best way to push Brother Sextus off course? There was no point in a preemptive opening, obviously, since South would have to go straight to game anyway. The Abbot decided to open one spade. If the worst happened and partner raised the suit, they should be able to scramble a few tricks.

Brother Sextus, sitting South, reckoned he had game values facing a Eustacian partner. Since spades had been called on his right, it seemed that hearts offered the best prospects. "Four hearts," he said, hoping to find a suitable dummy.

"Double!" said Brother Xavier, trusting that this call would escape criticism.

After two passes Brother Sextus paused to reconsider the position. The double of four hearts had been altogether too eager for his liking. Perhaps the Abbot's opening bid had been on a short suit, not an uncommon manoeuvre against a player with a Eustacian partner. Brother Sextus took a deep breath. "Four spades," he said, hoping he wasn't moving from a bad spot to a worse one.

Brother Xavier shrugged his shoulders. "Double," he said. No further bidding resulted. This had been the auction:

Brother Xavier's Indiscretion

South	West	North	East
Bro.	Bro.	Bro.	The
Sextus	Xavier	Anthony	Abbot
	No	No	1 ♠
4 ♡	Dble	No	No
4 ♠	Dble	No	No
No			

West led the queen of diamonds and Brother Sextus inspected the dummy exultantly. He won the diamond lead with the ace and cashed another trick in the suit, preparing for a cross-ruff. After taking the ace of hearts, he ruffed a heart with ♠ 7, East discarding a club. Six more red-suit ruffs followed in quick succession. Declarer's only loser was in the club suit.

"Yes, thank you, partner," said Brother Sextus. "A very suitable dummy. I suppose we should have been in six, but it was a difficult hand to bid."

Brother Xavier glanced apprehensively across the table. "I'm sorry, Abbot. Perhaps I should have left them in four hearts, instead of doubling. I certainly would have done if you'd opened the bidding in clubs, but . . ."

The Abbot silenced him with a wave of the hand and proceeded to calculate the score. "Brother Anthony would certainly have taken the right view on your hand," he observed, reaching once more for his wallet. "As it is, I make the damage 13 points."

It was the Abbot's turn to partner Brother Anthony. On the first hand of the rubber he dealt himself ♠ A Q 6 ♡ A 5 ◇ A K 10 3 ♣ A K 9 4. He looked across at Brother Anthony, who as usual was studying his hand impassively. What riches lay opposite, wondered the Abbot. Seven spades to the king and a minor suit queen? A balanced yarborough? The one certainty was that there were quite a few points to be made up. "Seven no-trumps," he declared firmly.

12

The Abbot and the Soup Bowl

The Abbot pinned a notice on the board opposite the refectory and there was soon a crowd of monks gathered round it.

THE FOLLOWING TEAM OF EIGHT WILL REPRESENT THE MONASTERY AGAINST ST. HILDA'S CONVENT FOR THE "MARTYR'S PLATTER".

'A' team.	The Abbot / Bro. Lucius
	Bro. Paulo / Bro. Xavier
'B' team.	Bro. Aelred / Bro. Michael
	Bro. Adam / Bro. Cameron

"Fame at last!" chuckled Brother Aelred. "I can't think why the Abbot selected me, though. I revoked against him last week."

"In the Martyr's Platter the 'B' team has to be below County Master rank," Brother Zac pointed out. "I suppose that rather narrows the field."

A week or two later the two teams assembled in a church hall halfway between the two establishments. The Abbot's first move put him against one half of the convent 'B' team.

"Spare no quarter here, Lucius," he said, as they approached the table. "Their top four will doubtless rip our 'B' team to pieces, so we must do the same." Assuming a friendly smile, he eased himself into the plush red chair. "Good afternoon, ladies," he said. "Nothing to fear from us; we're as simple as we look. Straight Acol, variable no-trump."

The more elderly of the two nuns peered at him from under her wimple. "Livorno Strong Diamond system with the multi," she informed them. "Vinje leads and signals throughout."

The Abbot rose to his feet. "I'm so sorry," he said. "I believe we must be at the wrong table. We should be playing your 'B' team."

The nun smiled. "Sister Ulrike and I returned only recently from ten years in the Congo," she said. "The Red and Green Beads we gained there aren't valid in this country, so the Reverend Mother was able to slip us into the 'B' team."

The Abbot and the Soup Bowl

N–S game, dealer South

	The Abbot ♠ K 9 8 5 ♡ K ◇ K Q 6 2 ♣ A J 9 8	
Sister Beatrice ♠ None ♡ J 10 9 8 7 6 5 2 ◇ 9 3 ♣ K 10 2	N W E S	*Sister Ulrike* ♠ J 7 6 4 2 ♡ Q 4 ◇ 10 8 4 ♣ Q 6 4
	♠ A Q 10 3 ♡ A 3 ◇ A J 7 5 ♣ 7 5 3 *Bro. Lucius*	

Brother Lucius opened one spade on the South cards and Sister Beatrice overcalled 1 NT.

"How strong is this 1 NT bid?" demanded the Abbot, peering over his glasses.

"16–18," replied Sister Ulrike.

"Double," said the Abbot.

Two passes followed and there was a brief pause as Sister Beatrice considered her next move. The Abbot studied his cards contentedly. Fancy this pair of old dears thinking they could hoodwink him and Lucius!

"Two no-trumps," said Sister Beatrice, folding her fan.

The Abbot shrugged his shoulders. If two elderly nuns wanted to bid like schoolboys, he would treat them like schoolboys. "Double," he said.

After two further passes, Sister Beatrice rescued herself to three hearts. The Abbot cue-bid four hearts and Brother Lucius, looking favourably on his three splendid aces, leapt to six spades. This had been the auction:

South	*West*	*North*	*East*
Bro. Lucius	Sister Beatrice	The Abbot	Sister Ulrike
1♠	1 NT	Dble	No
No	2 NT	Dble	No
No	3♡	4♡	No
6♠	End		

Brother Lucius won the heart lead in dummy and played a trump to the ace, exposing the 5–0 break. He next led a club to the 9 and queen, East returning the queen of hearts. A successful finesse of the club jack, followed by the ace of clubs and three rounds of diamonds, left this end position:

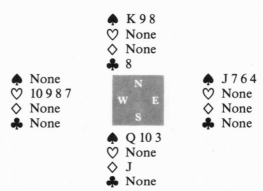

```
                 ♠ K 9 8
                 ♡ None
                 ◇ None
                 ♣ 8
 ♠ None                          ♠ J 7 6 4
 ♡ 10 9 8 7        N             ♡ None
 ◇ None        W       E         ◇ None
 ♣ None            S             ♣ None
                 ♠ Q 10 3
                 ♡ None
                 ◇ J
                 ♣ None
```

When the eight of clubs was led, East ruffed with the seven and Brother Lucius overruffed with the ten. It was now a simple matter to ruff his last diamond with the king and pick up East's jack of trumps.

"Yes, I should have sacrificed," said Sister Beatrice. "I can play in 1 NT doubled or seven hearts doubled. It makes no difference; they both cost 1100."

Across the room Brother Aelred and his partner were apprehensive as they faced Sister Grace and Sister Agnes of the convent 'A' team.

Game all, dealer South

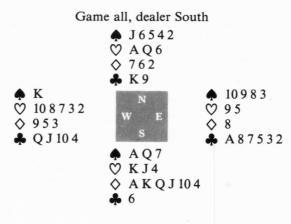

```
                 ♠ J 6 5 4 2
                 ♡ A Q 6
                 ◇ 7 6 2
                 ♣ K 9
 ♠ K                             ♠ 10 9 8 3
 ♡ 10 8 7 3 2      N             ♡ 9 5
 ◇ 9 5 3       W       E         ◇ 8
 ♣ Q J 10 4        S             ♣ A 8 7 5 3 2
                 ♠ A Q 7
                 ♡ K J 4
                 ◇ A K Q J 10 4
                 ♣ 6
```

The Abbot and the Soup Bowl

South	West	North	East
Sister	Bro.	Sister	Bro.
Grace	Michael	Agnes	Aelred
2 ◇	No	2 ♠	No
4 NT	No	5 ◇	No
6 ◇	End		

Brother Michael led the queen of clubs against six diamonds. When dummy went down, Sister Grace was disturbed to find no king of spades on view. The club ace was obviously offside, so she played low at trick 1. Clubs were continued and Sister Grace ruffed the second round.

The slam seemed to depend on East holding a doubleton or singleton king of spades. Sister Grace's first move was to run the entire trump suit, East throwing four clubs. Then she took three heart tricks, ending in dummy.

On the third round of hearts Brother Aelred, sitting East, had only spades remaining and therefore released ♠ 3. Sister Grace studied this card in learned fashion, then looked sharply at Brother Aelred. Why should he throw a spade? Surely even such a vacuous opponent as Brother Aelred would only do so from a four-card suit. Sister Grace realised that a spade finesse would be pointless in that case. Even if it succeeded, she would still have to give East the last trick. Boldly taking her only chance, she led a spade to the ace. The king appeared from a disbelieving Brother Michael, who had been holding his cards tightly to his chest, and Sister Grace claimed the contract.

"How did you know I didn't have the king?" asked a puzzled Brother Aelred.

"Well, when you discarded a spade I put you with four spades to your partner's one," replied Sister Grace.

"Oh, I see," replied Brother Aelred dubiously. But didn't that make it *more* likely that he had the king? He would have to look up the odds later in one of Brother's Lucius's books.

On the next round the Abbot found himself at the Mother Superior's table. This season the 84-year-old Sister Myrtle, a confirmed overbidder, had been harnessed to the Mother Superior in an effort to discipline her bidding.

E–W game, dealer North

```
                ♠ 8 7
                ♡ Q 8 4 2
                ◇ A K 10 6
                ♣ J 9 5
♠ A 9 6 5 3         N          ♠ Q J 10 4
♡ A K 5 3      W         E     ♡ 6
◇ J 5                         ◇ 9 7 4 2
♣ 7 2             S            ♣ Q 8 6 3
                ♠ K 2
                ♡ J 10 9 7
                ◇ Q 8 3
                ♣ A K 10 4
```

South	West	North	East
Mother	Bro.	Sister	The
Superior	Lucius	Myrtle	Abbot
		No	No
1 NT	No	2 ♣	No
2 ♡	No	4 ♡	End

Brother Lucius decided that his trump holding called for a forcing game. He therefore led the ace of spades against four hearts.

"Thank you, Sister Myrtle," said the Mother Superior as the dummy went down. "A raise to three hearts will be quite adequate next time you hold the hand."

Expecting the lead to be from the ace–king, the Abbot signalled his approval with the queen. Brother Lucius continued the suit and the Abbot was distinctly less pleased when the Mother Superior won with the king. A low trump to the queen was followed by a second trump, East showing out and West winning with the king. Brother Lucius pressed on with his spade attack and the Mother Superior ruffed in dummy, realising that the hand was running out of control. It seemed rather feeble to play for one down by switching her attention to the minor suits, so she led dummy's last trump in the vain hope that Brother Lucius had no spades remaining. Brother Lucius won with the ace and dislodged declarer's last trump with a fourth round of spades. The contract was now two down since he had a spade to cash when he scored his last trump.

The Abbot and the Soup Bowl

The Mother Superior turned to Brother Lucius. "I thought you'd helped me with that lead," she said, "but it seems it was the only one to break the contract."

At half-time the monastery team was just 5 IMPs in the lead. The contestants seated themselves for the traditional supper of leek and potato soup prepared by the nuns, wholemeal bread and St. Titus goat's-milk cheese.

"Exquisite cheese, Abbot, as always," said the Mother Superior.

"We have Brother Julius to thank for that," replied the Abbot. "Oh no, would you believe it? I seem to have spilt some soup on my cassock."

The Mother Superior looked across in concern. "Perhaps your soup bowl has a leek in it," she suggested.

"Oh, very good, Reverend Mother," tittered Sister Agnes.

The Abbot lifted the offending bowl and inspected it. "Difficult to tell in this light," he said. "It seems all right."

Battle was soon resumed. The first round after supper saw the two 'B' teams in opposition.

N–S game, dealer South

				♠ 6 3
				♡ A 9 5
				◇ Q 10 8 5 3
				♣ K 7 4

♠ K Q 10 8   ♠ 9 5 4
♡ 10 7 6 2   ♡ Q J 3
◇ J 7 4   ◇ K 9 6
♣ J 9   ♣ Q 10 6 2

♠ A J 7 2
♡ K 8 4
◇ A 2
♣ A 8 5 3

South	West	North	East
Bro.	Sister	Bro.	Sister
Aelred	Carol	Michael	Suzanne
1 NT	No	3 ◇	No
3 NT	End		

Brother Michael didn't like to raise directly to 3 NT with a low doubleton spade, so he marked time with three diamonds. This pointless manoeuvre was common practice in the monastery 5p game. The opener always rebid 3 NT and nobody thought anything strange about it.

Sister Carol, an 18-year-old novice, led the king of spades and Brother Aelred won in hand. Diamonds seemed the most promising source of tricks so he played ace and another diamond, finessing the ten. East won with the king and the defenders cashed three spade tricks. When the diamonds divided, Brother Aelred was able to claim the remainder for + 600.

"Could we have done any better?" asked Sister Carol with a shy smile.

"I think not, my dear," replied Brother Aelred. "The way I played it, the contract was undefeatable."

The hand was soon replayed in the 'A' team match.

South	West	North	East
The	Sister	Bro.	Sister
Abbot	Agnes	Lucius	Grace
1 NT	No	3 NT	End

Sister Agnes led the king of spades and her partner discouraged with the four. The Abbot followed with the seven, hoping to make East's four look like a peter. Unimpressed, Sister Agnes switched to a small heart. The Abbot won with the king and cashed the ace of diamonds, Sister Grace playing the nine in the East seat. The Abbot now needed four tricks from the diamond suit. If East's nine was from ◇ K 9 or ◇ 9 x, it could not be done, but if she held ◇ J 9 a diamond to the queen would win.

There seemed no point in any other play, so the Abbot led a diamond and called for dummy's queen. When Sister Grace won with the king and returned a spade, the contract could no longer be made. The Abbot put up the ace of spades and crossed to dummy in clubs to clear the diamonds. West won and exited safely in hearts to put him one down.

"Yes, the nine is an automatic false card from K 9 x," observed the Abbot knowledgeably. "That was my first thought when I saw it. Still, I had to play with the odds."

Across the room the other two 'A' team pairs were facing each other.

Love all, dealer South

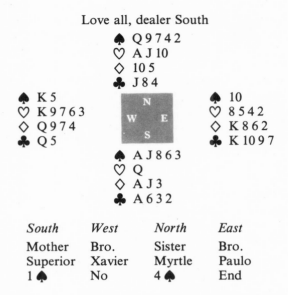

```
              ♠ Q 9 7 4 2
              ♡ A J 10
              ◇ 10 5
              ♣ J 8 4
♠ K 5                        ♠ 10
♡ K 9 7 6 3                  ♡ 8 5 4 2
◇ Q 9 7 4                    ◇ K 8 6 2
♣ Q 5                        ♣ K 10 9 7
              ♠ A J 8 6 3
              ♡ Q
              ◇ A J 3
              ♣ A 6 3 2
```

South	*West*	*North*	*East*
Mother	Bro.	Sister	Bro.
Superior	Xavier	Myrtle	Paulo
1 ♠	No	4 ♠	End

Brother Xavier, with no very inviting lead, placed the queen of clubs on the table.

"You will hardly criticise my four spade call this time," said the ancient Sister Myrtle as she tabled her cards.

The Mother Superior eyed the dummy disapprovingly but said nothing. She ducked the club lead and won the club continuation with the ace. She then crossed to the ace of hearts and led the queen of trumps. The ten appeared from East and the Mother Superior drew out the three. Pushing it back again, she paused to consider. Would West have led a doubleton queen of clubs, holding only a singleton trump? That seemed most unlikely.

Changing her plan, the Mother Superior overtook with the ace of trumps and exited to West's king, hoping that his return would aid her cause. This was the position:

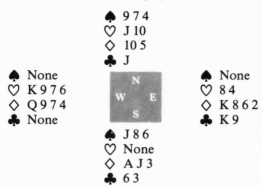

```
                ♠ 9 7 4
                ♡ J 10
                ◇ 10 5
                ♣ J
   ♠ None                       ♠ None
   ♡ K 9 7 6         N          ♡ 8 4
   ◇ Q 9 7 4     W     E        ◇ K 8 6 2
   ♣ None            S          ♣ K 9
                ♠ J 8 6
                ♡ None
                ◇ A J 3
                ♣ 6 3
```

When Brother Xavier played a diamond to the king and ace, declarer was able to establish a diamond trick for a club discard.

"Is it better if I exit with the queen of diamonds?" asked Brother Xavier. "A sort of Deschapelles Coup."

"No, I can just duck and finesse against your partner's king later," replied the Mother Superior, writing down the score in a neat hand.

"What if I try the king of hearts?" said Brother Xavier.

"No better, I think," replied Brother Paulo. "Declarer ruffs, crosses to a trump and leads diamond ten which I must cover to prevent two diamond tricks. Now Reverend Mother can throw a diamond on the heart winner and endplay you with diamond jack."

Sister Myrtle, who had given the impression of dozing off after putting down the dummy, stirred in her seat. "By that time, declarer's trumps would be exhausted," she said. "No, the king of hearts return does beat it. So would a low heart for that matter, but there's no point hanging in three, Reverend Mother. I'm sure you agree."

Play finished shortly after ten o'clock and it transpired that the convent had won the match by a handsome 35 IMPs. As was the custom, the velvet-lined box containing the relics of the Martyr's Platter was presented to the winning captain by the losing captain.

"Well played, Reverend Mother," said the Abbot, attempting a warm smile. "Your 'B' team was too good for us this year."

The Mother Superior took hold of the box and turned to address the contestants. "Some people would see the contents of this box as just a few worm-ridden pieces of wood," she said, opening the box and gazing down at its contents. "But to those of our persuasion they are a precious reminder of the blessed martyr, Edwina of Baddersley, whose courage in her final moments set us all such an inspiring example."

Trying hard to remember who Edwina of Baddersley was, the Abbot nodded his agreement. He looked round at the other monks to make sure they were following his example.

"There's something on the old boy's mind," whispered Brother Michael.

"So there jolly well should be," replied Brother Aelred. "How could anyone go off in that 3 NT with $\diamond$ Q 10 x x x? It's quite impossible."

PART II

Interlude in Africa

13

Battle in Bhumpopo City

From far away the wind carried the noise of drums beating. Brother Tobias, who was breakfasting in the open air, called the Witchdoctor to him. "What's the news this morning?" he asked. "Anything interesting?"

"Dey are Zbolwumba drums," the Witchdoctor him. "Dey say trials are being held for de team to represent Upper Bhumpopo in de African Championships. Dey suggestin' we enter a joint team with de Zbolwumbas."

"Nonsense!" exclaimed Brother Tobias, reaching for his third guava fruit, "There's no need to weaken our team with a Zbolwumba pair. We can enter with Brother Luke and Mbozi."

A few weeks later the Bozwambi team joined a colourful throng of contestants in the ballroom of the Bhumpopo Hilton. Play was soon under way.

N–S game, dealer East

```
                    Bro. Tobias
                    ♠ A Q 8 2
                    ♡ A K
                    ◇ Q 10 7 6 2
                    ♣ 7 5
   Pradap                                Majuba
   ♠ 6 5 3            N                   ♠ 4
   ♡ Q 7 2        W       E               ♡ 10 8 6 5 3
   ◇ 9 5 3            S                   ◇ K J 8 4
   ♣ A J 10 8                            ♣ 9 4 2
                    ♠ K J 10 9 7
                    ♡ J 9 4
                    ◇ A
                    ♣ K Q 6 3
                    Witchdoctor
```

[66]

"Neba ngotta," announced the East player, whose fearsome appearance was crowned with the purple headdress of the Jopzangda tribe.

"Dat meanin' *no bid*, Bwana," explained the Witchdoctor, sitting South.

"Do you mean some of these teams don't even speak English?" said Brother Tobias. "What an appalling state of affairs! Brother Luke and I will set up some classes for tomorrow morning."

Majuba turned towards Brother Tobias and inspected him as if he were some giant toad. "We will bid in English if you prefer," he said.

"Oh . . . you do speak English," said Brother Tobias with a nervous laugh.

"Yes. It was customary when I was at Trinity College, Cambridge."

This was the eventual auction:

South	West	North	East
Witch-	Pradap	Bro.	Majuba
doctor		Tobias	
			No
1 ♠	No	4 ♠	No
4 NT	No	5 ♡	No
6 ♠	End		

With any other partner Brother Tobias would have made a delayed game raise or even a jump shift. In the present circumstances a raise to four spades was sufficient. The Witchdoctor treated such raises to game as highly invitational, almost forcing, and since his hand was far from a minimum he advanced via Blackwood to the small slam.

A trump was led, won in the dummy, and the Witchdoctor continued with a club to the king and ace. Winning the trump return in hand, he noted that there were only two trumps in dummy to deal with three losers in hand. It was time to turn his attention to the diamond suit.

He cashed the ace of diamonds and crossed to dummy twice in hearts to ruff two diamonds. Queen of clubs and a club ruff left this end position, with the dummy on lead:

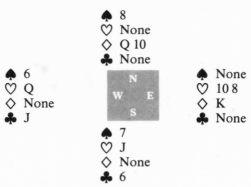

```
              ♠ 8
              ♡ None
              ◇ Q 10
              ♣ None
♠ 6                        ♠ None
♡ Q                        ♡ 10 8
◇ None                     ◇ K
♣ J                        ♣ None
              ♠ 7
              ♡ J
              ◇ None
              ♣ 6
```

Had the diamond king fallen in three rounds, the Witchdoctor could now have drawn the last trump, remaining in dummy. As it was, he ruffed a diamond with ♠ 7 and turned to observe Pradap, sitting West, who had not yet followed to the trick.

Pradap considered each card in turn. He could not afford the jack of clubs because his partner had shown three cards in the suit by following upwards. The Witchdoctor, meanwhile, began to flutter his eyelids and roll his eyes upwards so that only the whites were showing.

Pradap also ruled out an underruff, since dummy could then be reached with a ruff to score the established diamond. The Witchdoctor mouthed a silent incantation and began to rock his head from side to side.

Unaware of this, Pradap eventually decided to part with the heart queen in the hope that his partner held the jack.

"Snake-god be praised!" cried the Witchdoctor when the queen of hearts appeared. "Jmutmut evil eye makin' you throw de wrong card."

"Hah! Evil-eye don' worry de Jopzangda," replied Pradap. "It was run-of-de-mill squeeze. I havin' no card to spare."

A few hands later the Witchdoctor found himself in another tight contract.

Love all, dealer North

	♠ A K Q 2	
	♡ 3	
	◇ A 10 7 4	
	♣ Q J 9 4	

♠ 8 7 3		♠ J 10 5 4
♡ A 9 7 5 2		♡ K J 6
◇ J 6 5		◇ Q 9 2
♣ K 6		♣ 8 7 5

	♠ 9 6	
	♡ Q 10 8 4	
	◇ K 8 3	
	♣ A 10 3 2	

South	*West*	*North*	*East*
Witch-	Pradap	Bro.	Majuba
doctor		Tobias	
		1 ♠	No
2 ♣	No	4 ♣	No
5 ♣	End		

West led a diamond against five clubs and East's 9 forced the king. Crossing to a spade, the Witchdoctor led a heart from dummy. East went in with the king and returned a trump. The Witchdoctor won with the ace of trumps and cross-ruffed at high speed to produce this ending:

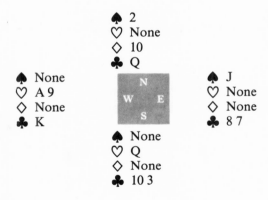

	♠ 2	
	♡ None	
	◇ 10	
	♣ Q	

♠ None		♠ J
♡ A 9		♡ None
◇ None		◇ None
♣ K		♣ 8 7

	♠ None	
	♡ Q	
	◇ None	
	♣ 10 3	

Dummy's spade was led and the Witchdoctor was disappointed to see East produce the last spade. Eventually he decided to ruff low and, as luck would have it, West had to overruff with the king and allow him to score his last two trumps separately.

When the board was replayed the opponents landed in three no-trumps:

South	West	North	East
Xhitu	Bro. Luke	Zubok	Mbozi
		1 ♣	No
1 ♡	No	1 ♠	No
1 NT	No	2 NT	No
3 NT	End		

Brother Luke led the 5 of hearts and Mbozi played the jack, taken by declarer's queen. When declarer crossed to a spade and led the club queen, Mbozi signalled with the 8 of clubs. The club finesse lost and Brother Luke continued hearts, the defenders picking up the remainder of the suit to put the contract one down.

"What a good card at trick 1, Mbozi!" exclaimed Brother Luke. "He makes it if you play the king."

"How did you know to continue de suit?" demanded the black-bearded Xhitu, flashing his eyes suspiciously.

"I was hoping you would ask that," said Brother Luke, well pleased with himself. "My partner's 8 of clubs was a Smith peter, showing a good holding in the suit originally led."

"Smitt peter?" said Xhitu. "Is dat licensed by de UBBU?"

The Bozwambi team scored well in the early matches and celebrated this achievement by doing full justice to the excellent tea provided. Their first game after the tea interval was against the Jahuzda Nomads.

"How are your buffalo herds this year?" enquired Brother Luke, biting into a kofta sausage that he had brought with him from the buffet table.

"Dey's always eatin' too much leaves of de Bonzyum bush," the Jahuzda chieftain informed him. "Upsets de buffalo's stomach and gives dem de runs."

Brother Luke looked at the remaining half of his sausage with distaste. "How interesting," he replied.

On the fourth board of the match against the Nomad team this slam hand arrived.

E–W game, dealer South

```
              ♠ 7 6 3
              ♡ K 10 8 5
              ◇ K 9 7
              ♣ 10 7 3
♠ 10 4              N              ♠ 9 2
♡ 9 6 4 3      W         E        ♡ 2
◇ Q 8 5 4                         ◇ A J 10 6 3 2
♣ K Q 8            S              ♣ J 6 4 2
              ♠ A K Q J 8 5
              ♡ A Q J 7
              ◇ None
              ♣ A 9 5
```

South	West	North	East
Chief	Mbozi	Mrazana	Bro.
Jbobo			Luke
1♣	No	1◇	No
2♠	No	3♠	No
4♣	No	4◇	No
4♡	No	4♠	No
5◇	No	5♡	No
6♠	End		

"We's playin' Jahuzda strong club," announced Chief Jbobo at the end of the auction. "Dat was epsilon relay sequence."

Mbozi led the king of clubs and the blue-clad cattle drover in the North seat put down the dummy.

"Where's de ace of diamonds?" demanded the chieftain, turning over the dummy's cards and looking underneath.

"I's cue-biddin' de king," explained Mrazana. "Dat's de modern style according to de white-bwana. He tellin' me about it in de tea-break."

"I does de tellin' in dis team," said the chieftain fiercely. "You have de ace next time or you's target practice for de young bowmen!"

The best chance of making this contract was to find East with a doubleton jack of clubs and the ace of diamonds. Then declarer could eliminate the major suits and exit in clubs, forcing East to concede a diamond trick. Such a play was beyond Chief Jbobo, who decided to duck the first trick. He won the club queen continuation and cashed ten tricks in the majors. At trick 12 South held the 9 of clubs and dummy the diamond king. Brother Luke, who had the ace of diamonds and jack of clubs remaining, could not decide which card to keep. Chief Jbobo lit an evil-smelling cheroot and puffed away at it, his hopes rising steadily as the seconds passed. Eventually Brother Luke threw the club.

"I's afraid you jus' made de second-best discard," sniggered the chieftain, facing his ♣ 9 triumphantly. "It turnin' out to be a 50% slam in de end!"

"I had a difficult decision there, Mbozi," said Brother Luke with a dignified air. "Perhaps the defence would have been easier if you'd followed the club king with a low club instead of the queen."

When the board was replayed, a different contract resulted:

South	West	North	East
Witch-	Karaq	Bro.	Ahaazi
doctor		Tobias	
2 ♠	No	2 NT	No
3 ♡	No	4 ♡	No
5 ♣	No	5 ♡	No
6 ♡	End		

Partnering the Witchdoctor, Brother Tobias declined to make a forward move with only two kings in his hand. Three sign-offs in a row managed to keep the Witchdoctor out of the grand and the club king was led.

The Witchdoctor won in hand and cashed the ace of trumps. Muttering to himself, he then led the queen of trumps, overtaking with the king. After ruffing a diamond in hand with the jack, he finessed dummy's 8 of trumps. The last trump was now drawn and he claimed the contract.

Brother Tobias scratched his head in bewilderment. How could such an atrocious bidder play the dummy so beautifully?

"Well done, indeed," he said. "You worked that out very quickly."

"Him easy magic," said the Witchdoctor. "Even de white-bwana mos' probably playin' it dat way."

The Bozwambi team were soon busy comparing scores.

"Plus 980," said Brother Tobias hopefully.

"Er . . . minus 980," said Brother Luke.

"What? They found the play of overtaking the queen of hearts?"

"Yes. Yes, that's what happened," said Brother Luke hastily. "Isn't that so, Mbozi?"

"I's not watchin' you playin' it, Bwana," replied Mbozi, crossing his big toes beneath the table.

The final match of the first day was a local derby against the Zbolwumbas, who had decided to enter a team on their own. An early board found Brother Tobias in 3 NT:

Love all, dealer South

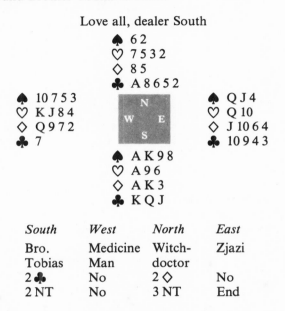

```
                    ♠ 6 2
                    ♡ 7 5 3 2
                    ◇ 8 5
                    ♣ A 8 6 5 2
♠ 10 7 5 3                          ♠ Q J 4
♡ K J 8 4          N                ♡ Q 10
◇ Q 9 7 2        W   E              ◇ J 10 6 4
♣ 7                S                ♣ 10 9 4 3
                    ♠ A K 9 8
                    ♡ A 9 6
                    ◇ A K 3
                    ♣ K Q J
```

South	West	North	East
Bro.	Medicine	Witch-	Zjazi
Tobias	Man	doctor	
2♣	No	2◇	No
2 NT	No	3 NT	End

The four of hearts was led to East's queen and declarer ducked. "Worth looking for a heart fit, wasn't it?" asked Brother Tobias absently.

The Witchdoctor shook his head scornfully. "Not with him holdin' king-jack to four."

The Zbolwumba medicine man edged his chair backwards and looked at the Witchdoctor with a new-found respect. Peeking was a highly regarded skill among the Zbolwumbas.

East returned the ten of hearts and declarer ducked again. West overtook and continued the suit, forcing declarer's ace. There was no hurry to test the clubs, so Brother Tobias led the nine of spades from hand. If West were to win this trick and cash the established heart, the count would be rectified and a squeeze might result.

As the cards lay, West was unable to take the trick without giving declarer three spade tricks. East won and returned the jack of diamonds. Brother Tobias captured this and played off five more winners, reducing the hand to this end position:

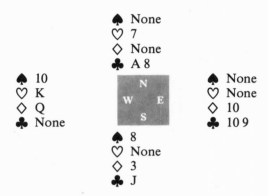

```
              ♠ None
              ♡ 7
              ◇ None
              ♣ A 8
  ♠ 10                        ♠ None
  ♡ K          N             ♡ None
  ◇ Q       W     E          ◇ 10
  ♣ None        S             ♣ 10 9
              ♠ 8
              ♡ None
              ◇ 3
              ♣ J
```

When Brother Tobias led the jack of clubs the Zbolwumba medicine man, sitting West, was reluctant to part with a card. Since a major-suit discard would definitely give declarer a trick, he threw the queen of diamonds, hoping for the best. Brother Tobias played low from dummy and threw East in on the next trick to give dummy the ace of clubs.

"Wasn't dat a grasshopper squeeze?" asked Zjazi. "De lead jumpin' to my hand and then to de dummy?"

"That is certainly the name the Bozwambi tribe use for it," replied Brother Tobias. "I believe a distinguished author in England called it a stepping-stone squeeze."

"White-bwana squeezin' me too," the medicine man informed his partner. "Hope our lads is awake in de other room or we mebbe losin' a swing on dis one."

"If I do lookin' for a fit in de majors," observed the Witchdoctor, "dey mos' probably leadin' a diamond. De play's not so easy on dat lead."

"It was hardly lay-down on the lead I received," replied Brother Tobias.

At the end of the first day's play the Bozwambi team led the 22-team field by a narrow margin. "What an honour if we could win these trials and represent Upper Bhumpopo," said Brother Luke as he sampled the rare luxury of a lager in the hotel bar.

"If we do win, I'm going to write a long letter back to the monastery," said Brother Tobias with a chuckle. "Imagine how pleased the Abbot would be if he heard we were internationals!"

14

The Witchdoctor's Farewell Gift

The Bozwambi team had spent a most comfortable night at the Bhumpopo Hilton. Since the hotel's rates were well beyond their means, the Witchdoctor had extracted a pass-key from one of the young chambermaids. The two missionaries had not enquired into the exact method of persuasion.

The four were therefore well rested when they began the defence of their overnight lead.

North–South game, dealer North

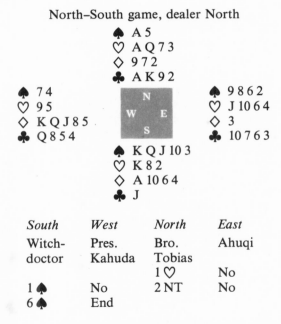

♠ A 5
♡ A Q 7 3
◇ 9 7 2
♣ A K 9 2

♠ 7 4
♡ 9 5
◇ K Q J 8 5
♣ Q 8 5 4

♠ 9 8 6 2
♡ J 10 6 4
◇ 3
♣ 10 7 6 3

♠ K Q J 10 3
♡ K 8 2
◇ A 10 6 4
♣ J

South	West	North	East
Witch-	Pres.	Bro.	Ahuqi
doctor	Kahuda	Tobias	
		1 ♡	No
1 ♠	No	2 NT	No
6 ♠	End		

West, an enormous African wearing a Western suit, led the king of diamonds. The Witchdoctor won immediately and drew four rounds of trumps. When he cashed the ace, queen and king of hearts, the suit failed to divide. This was the end position:

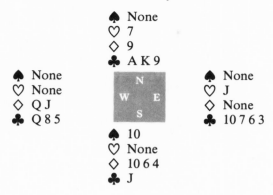

```
              ♠ None
              ♡ 7
              ◇ 9
              ♣ A K 9
♠ None                      ♠ None
♡ None                      ♡ J
◇ Q J                       ◇ None
♣ Q 8 5                     ♣ 10 7 6 3
              ♠ 10
              ♡ None
              ◇ 10 6 4
              ♣ J
```

The ten of spades was led and the large African eventually decided to retain his club guard, letting go a diamond. Dummy threw a diamond and East discarded a club. The Witchdoctor now led the jack of clubs, which was covered and won in the dummy. East was then thrown in with a heart and had to return a club into dummy's K–9.

"Excellent play, partner," chortled Brother Tobias. "You were lucky that West covered the jack of clubs, of course."

"Make no difference, Bwana," replied the Witchdoctor. "If he duck, I run de jack of clubs and put him in with a diamond. He mus' leadin' a club now."

"What if West comes down to two diamonds and two clubs and refuses to cover the jack of clubs?" persisted Brother Tobias.

To create a diversion, the Witchdoctor leapt four feet into the air to catch a spidery creature of the genus Melanchroi. "Him very good medicine for rheumatics," he remarked on his return to earth.

"Yes, that defence beats it," continued Brother Tobias, ignoring the Witchdoctor's antics. "Do you see?" he said, turning towards the overweight African. "You could have beaten it."

"Dat's quite impossible," declared East. "My partner never makin' any mistakes."

"Who was that fat bloke?" enquired Brother Tobias when the match was over. "He must weigh more than I do."

"You mos' unwise to criticizin' his play, Bwana," replied the Witchdoctor. "He de President of Upper Bhumpopo. Anyone annoyin' him mos' usually take a short swim in de crocodile river."

"I can hardly believe that applies to a British passport holder," replied Brother Tobias.

In the last match of the trials the Bozwambi team faced a team of doctors from the Bhumpopo City Hospital.

Love all, dealer South

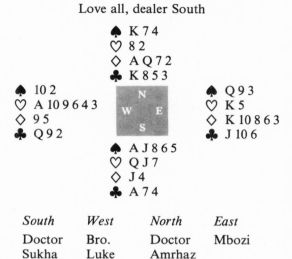

```
                    ♠ K 7 4
                    ♡ 8 2
                    ◇ A Q 7 2
                    ♣ K 8 5 3
    ♠ 10 2                          ♠ Q 9 3
    ♡ A 10 9 6 4 3                  ♡ K 5
    ◇ 9 5                           ◇ K 10 8 6 3
    ♣ Q 9 2                         ♣ J 10 6
                    ♠ A J 8 6 5
                    ♡ Q J 7
                    ◇ J 4
                    ♣ A 7 4
```

South	West	North	East
Doctor	Bro.	Doctor	Mbozi
Sukha	Luke	Amrhaz	
1 ♠	No	2 ♣	No
2 ♠	No	4 ♠	End

Brother Luke led the nine of diamonds and Dr. Sukha prescribed the two from dummy. Mbozi, who had played with great accuracy throughout the trials, won with the king and switched to the king of hearts. When West signalled with the ten, thoughts of a diamond ruff could be abandoned. A heart to the ace and a heart back promoted a trump trick for the defenders.

In the other room Brother Tobias had to struggle hard to keep the Witchdoctor out of a slam:

South	West	North	East
Witch-	Doctor	Bro.	Professor
doctor	Johrabi	Tobias	Baghassar
1 ♠	No	2 ◇	No
2 ♠	No	3 ♠	No
4 ♣	No	4 ♠	End

"I's a bit stick-in-de-mud today," said the Witchdoctor when he reluctantly decided not to advance over four spades.

Once again the 9 of diamonds was led, but the Witchdoctor called immediately for dummy's ace. A spade finesse was followed by the ace–king of trumps and a heart to the queen and ace. The club switch was taken in hand and the Witchdoctor cleared his diamond trick.

East returned another club but the Witchdoctor won on the table and discarded his club loser on the queen of diamonds. A second heart lead towards his hand established the tenth trick.

"Isn't it rather easier if you duck the first trick?" said Brother Tobias. "You'd have gone down if both hearts had been offside."

"He mos' probably leadin' de suit with de ace–king, Bwana," replied the Witchdoctor, marking his scorecard with an expensive-looking fountain pen. "And if I playin' in de way Bwana suggest . . . poof!"

On the very last hand of the event, an elegant bidding sequence put the Witchdoctor into six spades:

Game all, dealer West

♠ 6 5
♡ K J 6 4
◇ A K 8
♣ A K 7 4

♠ 3
♡ A 10 8 3
◇ Q J 9 6
♣ J 6 5 2

♠ 10 8 4
♡ Q 9 7
◇ 10 4 3 2
♣ Q 9 3

♠ A K Q J 9 7 2
♡ 5 2
◇ 7 5
♣ 10 8

South	West	North	East
Witch-	Doctor	Bro.	Professor
doctor	Johrabi	Tobias	Baghassar
	No	1 NT	No
6 ♠	End		

Dr. Johrabi led the queen of diamonds, which was taken in the dummy. The Witchdoctor now played a spade to the queen, re-entered dummy with a club and played a second spade to the jack, scowling at West when he showed out. He now cashed the spade ace and flashed a low heart on to the table. Convinced that his partner held the king of trumps, West jumped in with the ace of hearts and the Witchdoctor claimed the balance.

"Unbelievable, partner!" cried Professor Baghassar. "Why don't you play low on the heart? He must get it wrong."

"Yes, but I thought you had the king of trumps."

"You think he would go straight to six on ♠ A Q J x x x and at most a couple of queens?" demanded the Professor. "That would be a lunatic overbid!"

"Quite so," agreed Dr. Johrabi with a spread of the hands. "That's what made it all the more likely."

The Bozwambi team had won the trials by a substantial margin and were called to the stage to be congratulated by President Kahuda.

"M'hannah dessani ajoukat?" enquired the President as the team approached him. "Jehaz al nijal brakhouni."

"Is he asking who's the captain?" said Brother Tobias. "Let me through. I should be at the front."

"No, Bwana," replied Mbozi. "He sayin' he left his gold scorin' pen on our table. He wonderin' if mebbe we picked it up."

"Didn't I see the Witchdoctor with an unusual pen earlier on?" said Brother Tobias. "Anyhow, where is the Witchdoctor? Where's he gone?"

"He goin' upstairs with dat chambermaid, Bwana," replied Mbozi. "He tellin' me he got mos' excellent farewell present for her."

15

The Witchdoctor's Suggestion

"Show de tickets, please!" called the perspiring ticket inspector, edging his way through the crowded 3rd class railway compartment.

Financial considerations had forced the Bozwambi team to make their triumphant return from the trials in less than ideal circumstances. Brother Tobias was wedged between a fat native woman and three crates of sharp-beaked chickens that kept pecking at his cassock. The other three team members had been unable to find a seat.

The Witchdoctor leaned forward and whispered into Brother Tobias's ear. "Now dey's checked de tickets we can movin' into de 1st class," he suggested.

Brother Tobias gave a grunt of disapproval. "That would be exceedingly dishonest," he said.

"Exceeding comfortable too, Bwana," replied the Witchdoctor with a horrible toothless grin.

As the chickens showed no sign of abating their attack, Brother Tobias nodded his agreement. Pushing past the scramble of people fighting for his vacated seat, he joined the others in an otherwise empty 1st class compartment.

"Hah! This is de life!" exclaimed the Witchdoctor, sitting cross-legged on the comfortable blue seats. "If we put Bwana Luke's packin' case in de middle, we can havin' nice game of cards."

North–South game, dealer South

```
              ♠ K 8 3
              ♡ A Q 5 4
              ◇ Q J 4 2
              ♣ K Q
 ♠ J 4          N          ♠ Q 10 7 5
 ♡ J 10 6 2   W   E        ♡ 9 3
 ◇ 10 9 8 6     S          ◇ K
 ♣ 8 6 3                   ♣ 10 9 7 5 4 2
              ♠ A 9 6 2
              ♡ K 8 7
              ◇ A 7 5 3
              ♣ A J
```

South	West	North	East
Witch-	Mbozi	Bro.	Bro.
doctor		Tobias	Luke
1 NT	No	2 ♣	No
2 ♠	No	6 NT	End

Mbozi led the ten of diamonds against 6 NT and dummy went down, revealing the cruel duplication in clubs. There was no point contributing an honour from dummy, so the Witchdoctor played a low diamond, giving a sniff of pleasure when East's king appeared.

His next move was a spade to the 8. East won with the ten and returned a club to the table. The king of spades dropped West's jack and the Witchdoctor continued with a spade to the 9, baring his yellow teeth triumphantly when the finesse succeeded. When the black aces were cashed, West was forced to unguard one of the red suits, giving declarer a twelfth trick.

"Why did you finesse on the third round of spades?" enquired Brother Tobias. "Mbozi could easily have held Q J x."

"Much more likely he holdin' J x," replied the Witchdoctor, gathering the cards and riffle-shuffling them with his gnarled fingers. "With Q J x he mebbe play de queen on de previous round."

"What's that to do with it?" said Brother Luke. "When I follow with the 7 on the third round there's only one card out, the queen. Quite obviously the odds are evens as to who holds the missing card."

"Don' think so, Bwana," said Mbozi. "De Principle of Restricted Choice applyin', isn't it?"

"Be quiet, both of you!" commanded Brother Tobias. "Brother Luke and I know what we're talking about. The odds are obviously evens."

The Witchdoctor glanced sullenly at the two missionaries. "Bwana Luke should winnin' de first spade with de queen, anyway," he muttered. "Dat might make me misguessin'."

The train rattled on through the sparse countryside, scattering a herd of wildebeest that had been grazing near the line. A few hands later the Witchdoctor was in another tricky contract.

Love all, dealer East

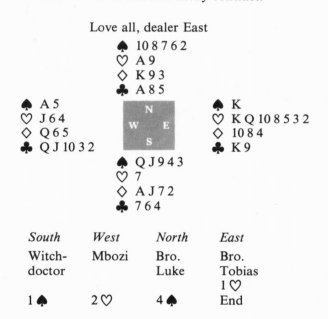

♠ 10 8 7 6 2
♡ A 9
◇ K 9 3
♣ A 8 5

♠ A 5
♡ J 6 4
◇ Q 6 5
♣ Q J 10 3 2

♠ K
♡ K Q 10 8 5 3 2
◇ 10 8 4
♣ K 9

♠ Q J 9 4 3
♡ 7
◇ A J 7 2
♣ 7 6 4

South	West	North	East
Witch-doctor	Mbozi	Bro. Luke	Bro. Tobias
			1 ♡
1 ♠	2 ♡	4 ♠	End

Mbozi led the queen of clubs against four spades and the Witchdoctor ducked in dummy. East overtook and returned the suit, dummy's ace winning the trick. The Witchdoctor, munching a betel nut in disgusting fashion, now ruffed out the hearts and led the queen of spades from hand. Mbozi covered with the ace, dropping his partner's king, and the Witchdoctor cackled with laughter, almost choking himself on the nut.

Mbozi cashed his club winner and exited with his remaining trump. The Witchdoctor won in dummy and eventually went one down when the diamond finesse failed.

"A lucky escape, partner," said Brother Tobias severely. "I trust it won't happen again."

"White-bwana talkin' through hat as usual," muttered Mbozi. "If I don' goin' in with de trump ace, he can't fail to makin' de contract."

"Do you know, I believe Mbozi's right," said Brother Luke. "If you win the trump king and return a diamond, declarer can throw dummy's club loser on the fourth round of diamonds."

"And if you returnin' a heart," said Mbozi, "he throwin' a club from hand and ruffin' in de dummy. Club ruff now and he puttin' me in with trump ace to open de diamonds."

"Hah!" declared the Witchdoctor. "Dat was some defence, Mbozi. You like finish my betel nut?"

The train ground to a halt and Mbozi poked his head out of the window to investigate. "Water buffalo on de line," he reported.

"Hardly worth stopping the train for a few water buffalo," commented Brother Tobias. "If the train went ahead at full speed, they'd soon learn not to stand there."

A railway official passed down the corridor and Brother Tobias slid open the door to call after him. "I say! Get those buffalo moving, will you? We have a connection to make at Khralbazula Junction."

"Me not buffalo shooer!" replied the affronted official. "Me de 1st class ticket inspector!"

Brother Tobias gave him a glassy smile. "So sorry to have troubled you," he said.

16

The Temptation of Brother Tobias

The Bhumpopo Express pulled round the long curve into Bozwambi junction and rolled to a halt amid much hissing of steam.

"Bozwambi Junction! Bozwambi Junction!" cried the Station Master, waving his baton importantly.

Mjubu was waiting to meet the victorious Bozwambi team. "Mos' heartiest congratulations, Bwana," he said, tossing Brother Tobias's luggage into the back of the Jeep. "We hearin' about your great win on de news-drums yesterday."

"Mind out with my luggage!" cried Brother Tobias. "Our prizes are in there. Some crystal decanters and glasses."

Since the African Championships, for which they had qualified, were due to be held in Tunis in only two months time, the Bozwambi team set up a series of practice matches against local opposition. The first of these encounters was against the much-improved Bozwambi Ladies Team.

Game all, dealer South

```
                    ♠ K 10 8 5 4 2
                    ♡ 6
                    ◇ K Q
                    ♣ J 7 6 2
    ♠ Q 9 3                         ♠ J 7 6
    ♡ K J 5             N           ♡ A 9 8 7 4 2
    ◇ J 10 9 7 4 3 2  W   E         ◇ 6
    ♣ None               S          ♣ Q 8 3
                    ♠ A
                    ♡ Q 10 3
                    ◇ A 8 5
                    ♣ A K 10 9 5 4
```

South	West	North	East
Bro.	Miss	Witch-	Mrs.
Tobias	Nabooba	doctor	Okoku
1 ♣	No	1 ♠	No
3 ♣	No	4 ♣	No
4 ◇	No	5 ♣	End

Miss Nabooba, whose slender figure was swathed in lime green, led the ten of diamonds against five clubs and the Witchdoctor laid out the dummy.

"Four trumps and a heart control, partner?" queried Brother Tobias. "Surely you can say more on those cards?"

The Witchdoctor shrugged his shoulders noncommittally. The diamond lead was taken by dummy's queen, and a trump to the ace confirmed that there was no trump loser.

"Yes, a slam swing away on this one, partner," announced Brother Tobias. "We can't afford this extravagance in Tunis. Surely you were worth four hearts over four diamonds?"

Brother Tobias returned to dummy's king of diamonds, intending to finesse in trumps. Mrs. Okoku ruffed and underled her ace of hearts for West to give her another diamond ruff. The club game was one down.

"Mebbe I should passin' three clubs, Bwana," suggested the Witchdoctor. "Seems we gettin' too high on dat one."

"Don't be impertinent," replied Brother Tobias. "Eleven tricks were cast-iron simply by cashing a second high trump. Since the lead of the ten of diamonds marked East with the jack, it seemed quite safe to go for the overtrick."

"My ten lead promised de jack, Bwana," Miss Nabooba informed him. "We's tryin' out Roman leads tonight."

"Oh, thank you so much for telling me," said Brother Tobias heavily. "Yes, very kind to point it out so promptly, just when I've sent a vulnerable game down the chute."

"Why take de risk, anyhow, Bwana?" asked the Witchdoctor.

"If you'll just listen, I might find the patience to explain it to you," said Brother Tobias. "Now, even if West is playing Roman leads, the chance of diamonds being 7-1 is about 2 or 3 per cent. Right? So, are you telling me I should give up 1 IMP for the overtrick 98% of the time, just to safeguard 13 IMPs 2% of the time? Does that make sense?"

"It makin' better sense to play de queen of hearts at trick 3," replied the Witchdoctor. "Still collectin' de overtrick if diamonds aren't 7-1, and you don't goin' off if dey are. Him Scissors Coup," he added, holding up his fists with the two first fingers crossed. "Cuts off de entries."

Meanwhile, across the jungle clearing in another hut, Mrs. Lzboto was at the helm in an awkward slam.

East–West game, dealer West

♠ K 7 5
♡ A 7 6 2
◇ A 5 3
♣ 10 6 3

♠ Q 9 2
♡ J 5
◇ K Q J 9 7 6 4
♣ 5

♠ 10 8 6 3
♡ Q 10 9 4
◇ 10 2
♣ J 7 2

♠ A J 4
♡ K 8 3
◇ 8
♣ A K Q 9 8 4

South	West	North	East
Mrs.	Mbozi	Mrs.	Bro.
Lzboto		El-Djem	Luke
	3 ◇	No	No
5 ♣	No	6 ♣	End

Mbozi led the king of diamonds and Mrs. Lzboto, usually a sharp dummy player, surveyed the dummy's assets. Eleven tricks were on view, and a twelfth would follow if the hearts divided or the queen of spades was onside. But what if East held four or more hearts and West the spade queen? Mrs. Lzboto fingered her necklace of turquoise beads thoughtfully. Yes, surely there would then be a double squeeze; with each defender guarding one red suit, neither could hold the spades.

"Play de 3," said Mrs. Lzboto.

Mrs. El-Djem looked up sharply. Was the word 'please' out of fashion?

"Yes, de 3," repeated Mrs. Lzboto.

Mbozi continued with a second diamond which declarer won in the dummy, discarding a heart from hand. After drawing trumps, Mrs. Lzboto tested the heart suit, ruffing the third round in hand. They failed to divide but now she ran the trump suit, leading her last trump to this end position:

[86]

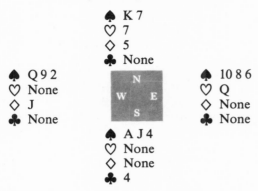

```
              ♠ K 7
              ♡ 7
              ◇ 5
              ♣ None
 ♠ Q 9 2                    ♠ 10 8 6
 ♡ None         N          ♡ Q
 ◇ J       W       E       ◇ None
 ♣ None         S          ♣ None
              ♠ A J 4
              ♡ None
              ◇ None
              ♣ 4
```

Each defender in turn had to release a spade, so the contract was assured whoever held the spade queen.

"Hah! De spade queen was offside!" exclaimed Mrs. Lzboto. "We mebbe gettin' nice swing on dis one."

"Mrs. Lzboto," reprimanded Brother Luke. "Surely we can manage a little more dignity? Bridge is meant to be a civilised game, is it not?"

"Hah! You jus' annoyed cos I makin' it," replied Mrs. Lzboto.

Mbozi eyed Mrs. Lzboto approvingly. Here was a woman after his own heart – plenty of spirit and a fine turn of phrase.

Much to the annoyance of Brother Tobias, the result of the match was a 19 IMP win for the Bozwambi Ladies.

"Don' worry, Bwana," said Miss Nabooba, slipping her arm round Brother Tobias's waist. "Even de muddiest pond has a silver fish in it."

"What's that supposed to mean?" grunted Brother Tobias.

"Well, a third pair would be mos' useful in Tunis, Bwana," said Miss Nabooba, pressing her slender form against him as she whispered in his ear. "Really it would. And I've always wanted to be an international."

The Witchdoctor's Lament

Brother Tobias was nearing the end of a heavy supper when the Witchdoctor entered the hut, his eyes flashing evilly.

"M'hazdrubah hotta! M'hazdrubah hou!" exclaimed the Witchdoctor, waving his wand of chicken feathers over Brother Tobias's head.

"Have I earned your displeasure in some way?" enquired Brother Tobias, reaching for the buffalo milk cheese.

"M'hazdrubah hesset! M'hazdrubah haglabah!" persisted the Witchdoctor, emitting a powerful odour.

"Your spells will have little effect on me, I assure you," said Brother Tobias. "Presumably you object to Miss Nabooba and Mrs. Okoku coming along as a third pair to the African Champsionships. It makes no difference; my mind is made up. They are due here shortly, in fact, for a practice game."

Brother Tobias was just lighting the large oil-lamp hanging from the ceiling, when the other three players arrived, Miss Nabooba wearing an alarmingly short cotton dress. Brother Tobias averted his eyes. Such temptations were quite unfair on such a humid evening.

"Clear these supper things away, will you, Mbozi," he said. "Then we can get straight on with the game."

Love all, dealer North

```
              ♠ A J 10
              ♡ J 9 7 2
              ◇ A 5 2
              ♣ A 8 5
♠ 7 6 4                        ♠ K Q 9 2
♡ 6            N               ♡ 8 4
◇ Q 10 9 6   W   E             ◇ K J 7
♣ K Q 10 7 2   S              ♣ 9 6 4 3
              ♠ 8 5 3
              ♡ A K Q 10 5 3
              ◇ 8 4 3
              ♣ J
```

The Witchdoctor's Lament

South	West	North	East
Bro.	Mrs.	Mbozi	Miss
Tobias	Okoku		Nabooba
		1 NT	No
4 ♡	End		

Mrs. Okoku led the king of clubs against four hearts. Brother Tobias won in the dummy and ruffed a club. After two rounds of trumps he ruffed the dummy's last club and led a low diamond from hand.

Mrs. Okoku, sitting West, could see that the defence would need two diamond tricks and two spade tricks to break the game. It was equally clear that both diamond tricks would have to be won on her side of the table, so that dummy's spades could be attacked successfully. She therefore inserted the nine of diamonds to prevent declarer ducking the trick to East.

Brother Tobias won with dummy's ace and Miss Nabooba was quick to dispense with her diamond king. None too pleased at these developments, Brother Tobias returned to hand with a trump and led the four of diamonds towards the dummy's 5-2.

Mrs. Okoku was not deceived by this manoeuvre. She played the ten, a mini Crocodile Coup, to swallow her partner's seven, and switched to a spade. The finesse lost and East returned the jack of diamonds to her partner's queen. Another spade from West defeated the contract.

"I's rather surprised you didn' try three no-trumps on your hand, Bwana," remarked Mrs. Okoku. "Mos' temptin', I mus' say. Particularly as you don' even playin' transfers."

"What does Mbozi know about transfers?" retorted Brother Tobias. "I might have bid three hearts, I suppose, but the contract would have been the same."

The hands ticked by with little in the way of incident until, some hours later, Brother Tobias found himself at the helm of another tricky heart game.

Interlude in Africa

East–West game, dealer South

```
            ♠ K 9 7 5 4
            ♡ A 8 4 3
            ◇ J 7 5 2
            ♣ None
♠ Q J 10 3              ♠ 8 2
♡ K Q 10        N      ♡ J 5
◇ 8          W     E   ◇ A 9 6 3
♣ J 9 6 5 2     S      ♣ K Q 8 4 3
            ♠ A 6
            ♡ 9 7 6 2
            ◇ K Q 10 4
            ♣ A 10 7
```

South	West	North	East
Bro.	Mrs.	Mbozi	Miss
Tobias	Okoku		Nabooba
1 NT	No	2♣	No
2♡	No	4♡	End

Mrs. Okoku led the queen of spades and Mbozi displayed the three-suited dummy.

"Only eight points?" grunted Brother Tobias. "I thought we played a weak no-trump at this vulnerability."

"Quite so, Bwana," replied Mbozi earnestly. "Vulnerable I would biddin' four clubs to show de club void."

Brother Tobias studied the dummy thoughtfully. Should he duck a round of trumps and then play the ace, leaving the enemy master trump at large? No, that would be dangerous here. When he subsequently forced out the ace of diamonds, the defenders might be able to play a third round of trumps.

Brother Tobias won the spade lead in hand, ruffed a club and then led a diamond from the table. When Miss Nabooba played low, he won with the king, ruffed a second club and continued with ace and another trump. As luck would have it, trumps were 3–2, so he was able to claim the contract, conceding two trumps and a diamond.

"Mos' difficult defence to find, partner, I's admittin'," declared Mrs. Okoku, "but you can beatin' de contract if you goin' up with de ace of diamonds."

"Yes, indeed," agreed Brother Tobias, with a sharp glance in Miss Nabooba's direction. "You had the chance of a diamond ruff, there."

"Hah! Fat lot of good dat would be with me holdin' de three trumps," observed Mrs. Okoku. "No, when you takin de ace of diamonds, you mus' playin' a second round of spades. Declarer now right in de soup bucket. If he duckin' a trump, I can promotin' your jack of hearts. If he playin' ace and another trump, I can pullin' a third round."

"In with de ace of diamonds and playin' another spade?" chuckled Miss Nabooba. "Dat would be some defence, I mus' say."

"All the same, we can't afford to miss chances like that when we play in Tunis," said Brother Tobias, rising sternly to his feet and bumping his head on the oil-lamp. "Shall we call it a day? It's past eleven and I have to be up early in the morning."

Miss Nabooba and Mrs. Okoku were walking back to their huts in the moonlight when they heard a rustling noise from a nearby bush.

"Ssh!" whispered Mrs. Okoku. "It mebbe a leopard!"

The bush parted and a fearsome creature leapt out at them from the darkness.

"M'hazdrubah hotta! M'hazdrubah hesset!" hissed the Witch-doctor, waving his chicken-feather wand over their heads.

"Don' thinkin' it's a leopard," said Miss Nabooba casually. "Dey don' usually havin' feathers, as a rule."

18

A Date in Tunis

After an arduous two-week journey the Bozwambi team arrived in Tunis, where they were due to represent Upper Bhumpopo in the African Championship. Funds were scarce, so they were obliged to take rooms in the Arab quarter near the perfume souk.

"You like nice bottle musk oil?" asked a gold-toothed Berber, tugging at the sleeve of Brother Tobias's cassock. "Only 12 dinars. No girl can resist when you wear it."

"I thank you, no," replied Brother Tobias, shaking himself free from the salesman's grasp.

"OK. For you I make special price," continued the Berber, running after them. "Just 5 dinars . . . or, OK, two bottles for 4 dinars."

They arrived at the Alexandria Hotel to find that their first match would be against Egypt, one of the stronger teams.

N–S game, dealer South

```
                    ♠ K
                    ♡ K J 8 3
                    ◇ Q 7 6 2
                    ♣ J 8 6 3
  ♠ Q 10 5 4 2                      ♠ J 9 7 6
  ♡ 2                               ♡ Q 5
  ◇ K 10 5 4 3          N          ◇ J 9
  ♣ A 9             W       E       ♣ K 10 5 4 2
                        S
                    ♠ A 8 3
                    ♡ A 10 9 7 6 4
                    ◇ A 8
                    ♣ Q 7
```

South	West	North	East
Witch-doctor	Wahid Shafel	Bro. Tobias	Adel Razah
1 ♡	1 ♠	2 ♡	4 ♠
5 ♡	End		

The Witchdoctor, having taken the push to five hearts, won the spade lead in dummy. After drawing trumps, he led a club to the queen and ace. West exited safely with a spade to the ace, and the Witchdoctor continued with the 7 of clubs to the 9, jack and king.

East's diamond switch was too late. The Witchdoctor won with the ace and crossed to dummy with a spade ruff to take a ruffing finesse with dummy's 8–6 of clubs. When East declined to cover, the Witchdoctor discarded a diamond and claimed the contract.

East clicked his fingers in annoyance. "I can beat this," he said. "If I rise with the king of clubs and come through a diamond, he is finished."

In the other room the Egyptian South preferred to double Mbozi in four spades and a 300 penalty resulted.

The Egyptian team led by 2 IMPs at the interval and Brother Tobias brought in the two ladies for the second half.

E–W game, dealer South

♠ A Q J
♡ 7 6 2
◇ 10 6 4
♣ 9 7 6 3

♠ 8 3
♡ J 10 9 3
◇ J 9 5
♣ K Q J 4

♠ K 10 9 6 5 4 2
♡ None
◇ A K
♣ 10 8 5 2

♠ 7
♡ A K Q 8 5 4
◇ Q 8 7 3 2
♣ A

South	West	North	East
Tekel El Habib	Miss Nabooba	Abdul Aziz	Mrs. Okoku
1 ♡	No	1 NT	3 ♠
4 ♡	End		

Miss Nabooba, who was wearing an extremely low-cut dress in her favourite green silk, led the king of clubs against four hearts. As the elderly bald-headed declarer inspected the dummy, Miss Nabooba leaned forward in the hope of distracting him.

"Small, please," said declarer, oblivious to her antics.

What a pity North isn't declarer, thought Miss Nabooba, giving him a friendly smile. He seems interested enough.

"Small please, I said!" reprimanded the declarer. Winning the club lead in hand, he drew three rounds of trumps and crossed to the ace of spades. He then led a diamond towards his hand, Mrs. Okoku winning with the ace and exiting in clubs.

Tekel El Habib ruffed in hand and paused for thought. The bidding, particularly the lack of a final double from West, marked East with the diamond king. And since East's spade suit was not too powerful, it seemed she was more likely to have found a vulnerable three-level call with 7–0–2–4 distribution rather than 7–0–3–3. Deciding this was the only clue available, declarer continued with a low diamond from hand, claiming the contract when East's king appeared.

"Oh dear! What useful clubs you had for me, partner," exclaimed Mrs. Okoku, fanning herself with her score-card. "With de spade ace onside, I can makin' four spades!"

"You can't reachin' my hand, can you?" replied Miss Nabooba. "If you try to cross in de club suit, South makin' his singleton trump."

When the hand was replayed, West raised his partner to four spades, expecting the three-level overcall to be based on a very good suit:

South	West	North	East
Witch-	Wahid	Bro.	Adel
doctor	Shafel	Tobias	Razah
1 ♡	No	1 NT	3 ♠
4 ♢	4 ♠	Dble	End

Razah, the youngest player in the Egyptian team, ruffed the ace of hearts lead. He could afford two trump losers, so it seemed to him that there was no need to lead the first round of spades from dummy. A low spade from hand would reduce the risk of a club ruff and would also gain if North had doubled on Q J x, South holding the singleton ace.

Declarer therefore led the two of spades from hand at trick 2 and subsequently entered dummy with a club to lead successfully towards his king of spades.

"What's dis double of four spades?" queried the Witchdoctor, rolling his bloodshot eyes at Brother Tobias. "Five diamonds only one down and we gettin' pathetic –790 instead."

"It was a cooperative double, partner," replied Brother Tobias loftily. "I'm surprised you left it in with a three-loser hand."

The Bhumpopo team had lost their first match by 16 VPs to 4 and surveyed the giant scoreboard disconsolately.

"Well, we're not last," said Brother Luke. "In fact we're 9 points ahead of the team from Benguela. They lost 20 to – 5."

The next match was imminent and Brother Tobias gathered the team around him. "We must set our sights on nothing less than first place," he declared. "That director over there, the one in the grass skirt, told me that this year's winners will play in the Bermuda Bowl."

"Really, Bwana?" said Miss Nabooba. "I always wanted to play in dat."

The Bozwambi team were apprehensive as they approached their next opponents, four athletic six-footers seated at a corner table.

"They are Jahamid tribe, Bwana!" exclaimed the Witchdoctor.

"Good, that's our right table," said Brother Tobias, inspecting the assignment card.

"De game is off! Bozwambi tribe never speak to Jahamid. Dey spearin' to death our great chief Bog-Hakub."

"Oh dear, that wasn't very nice of them," said Brother Luke sympathetically. "But when did all this happen? I've never heard of the gentleman in question."

"It written on de history-stones," replied the Witchdoctor. "Anyone speakin' to Jahamid get burnt to cinder immediately by Lightning-god."

"Dat's right, Bwana," said a wide-eyed Mbozi. "Everybody knowin' dat."

Brother Tobias could hide his exasperation no longer. Had they travelled 800 miles just to score 4 VPs in the first match and 0 in the second?

"Don't you worry, Bwana," said Mrs. Okoku bravely. "You play with Bwana Luke and I play with Miss Nabooba. We use biddin' boxes and no speak to dem."

Interlude in Africa

E–W game, dealer South

```
            ♠ 7 6 5
            ♡ 9 6 4
            ◇ Q 8 3
            ♣ K J 7 4
♠ 9 4                        ♠ K 8 3 2
♡ 8 7 3          N          ♡ 10 2
◇ J 10 9 2    W     E       ◇ A K 6 5
♣ 9 8 6 2        S          ♣ A 10 5
            ♠ A Q J 10
            ♡ A K Q J 5
            ◇ 7 4
            ♣ Q 3
```

South	West	North	East
Bro.	Garam	Bro.	Jupwallah
Tobias	Jdodo	Luke	
1 ♡	No	1 NT	No
2 ♠	No	3 ♡	No
4 ♡	End		

West, whose finely waved hair was smarmed down with coconut oil, led the jack of diamonds against four hearts. Declarer played low in dummy and the defenders pressed on with two more rounds of diamonds.

Dummy was woefully short of entries to finesse the spades, so Brother Tobias decided to ruff high on the third round of diamonds, hoping to drop a doubleton ten of trumps later. West followed suit on the diamond and Brother Tobias continued with two high trumps, feeling there was some justice in the world when the ten fell from East. These cards remained:

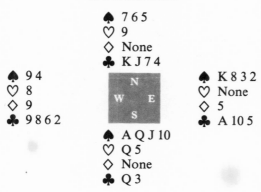

```
              ♠ 7 6 5
              ♡ 9
              ◇ None
              ♣ K J 7 4
♠ 9 4                          ♠ K 8 3 2
♡ 8          ┌─────────┐       ♡ None
◇ 9          │    N    │       ◇ 5
♣ 9 8 6 2    │  W   E  │       ♣ A 10 5
             │    S    │
             └─────────┘
              ♠ A Q J 10
              ♡ Q 5
              ◇ None
              ♣ Q 3
```

The queen of clubs was now run, ducked by East, and a club to the jack and ace left East with three unpalatable choices. A spade or a club would allow declarer an extra spade finesse, and on a diamond return declarer would ruff in dummy and discard a spade from hand. Tapping the ash from his cigarette onto Brother Luke's scorecard, East eventually opted for a spade. Declarer finessed successfully and crossed to the 9 of trumps. After discarding a spade on dummy's club winner, he finessed again in spades for his contract.

"I thought for a moment you'd forgotten to draw the third round of trumps," Brother Luke remarked brightly.

Brother Tobias, who had expected a word of praise for his efforts, moved his lips in silent prayer.

In the other room the diminutive ladies were tackling the taller Jahamid pair, each nearly seven feet high.

N–S game, dealer North

```
            ♠ 9 3
            ♡ A J 9 7 6 2
            ◇ K 5
            ♣ K 9 4
♠ 8 2            N            ♠ 10 6 4
♡ Q 10                       ♡ 5 3
◇ Q J 10 8 6 2  W     E      ◇ 9 4
♣ A 10 5         S           ♣ J 8 7 6 3 2
            ♠ A K Q J 7 5
            ♡ K 8 4
            ◇ A 7 3
            ♣ Q
```

South	West	North	East
	Mrs.	Jozo	Miss
Mahottah	Okoku	Bfudha	Nabooba
		1 ♡	No
2 ♠	No	3 ♡	No
4 NT	No	5 ◇	No
6 ♠	End		

Mrs. Okoku led the queen of diamonds and Mahottah won in dummy, East playing the 4. Declarer led a club next, to the queen and ace, and West returned another diamond to declarer's ace.

Mahottah now had two lines to consider. He could either hope to negotiate a diamond ruff without mishap or he could draw trumps and try to pick up the heart suit. Ruffing a diamond was not without its risks since West, leading from a sequence, was likely to have the longer holding. But dummy's 9 of trumps increased the attractions of this line, reducing the risk of an overruff.

Mahottah drew one round of trumps and marked further time by cashing the king of hearts. When the queen remained in hiding, he drew a deep breath and ruffed his last diamond with the 9. With an apologetic smile Miss Nabooba overruffed.

"Bafaqhassar!" exclaimed Mahottah, ruffing the club return and slumping in his chair as he conceded one down. "How were de hearts?"

"Queen-ten doubleton on de left, of course," replied his partner. "Dat's obvious when de ten shows, isn't it? If de ten was singleton she would leadin' it at trick 1."

Mahottah sent a withering glance across the table. "With an ace in hand you think she would leadin' a singleton against a slam? Let's hope it's not played in hearts in de other room."

The two ladies returned at half-time to find Brother Tobias sporting a rather sheepish expression.

"Did you play de big hand in spades or hearts, Bwana?" asked Miss Nabooba excitedly.

"Er . . . in hearts," replied Brother Tobias. "Unfortunately we had an accident in the bidding. West put in a nuisance bid of five diamonds over my Blackwood call and Brother Luke chose to double."

"But that's the right bid," protested Brother Luke. "Pass would show no aces and . . ."

"Yes, yes. So you told me at the time," interrupted Brother Tobias. "Anyhow, thinking there were two aces opposite, I bid seven hearts."

Miss Nabooba bit her lip but said nothing. What a pathetic waste of their good board.

"Still, it could have been worse," continued Brother Tobias. "We did at least get a diamond lead."

Miss Nabooba snatched his scorecard. "Unbelievable!" she cried. "You playin' joke with us. Plus 2210!"

A faraway look came into Mrs. Okoku's eyes. "This day will be written on de Bozwambi history-stones," she murmured. "At last, after over five hundred moons, de mos' horrible death of Bog-Hakub has been avenged."

19

Brother Tobias on Vu-Graph

Four consecutive wins in the African Championship had brought the Upper Bhumpopo team into third place at the half-way stage. Their clash against Morocco, lying second, was to be featured on Vu-Graph.

The noisy hall was packed as the tall bald-headed commentator from England, Rupert Treacher, took his seat at the microphone. The first hand was lifted into position on the Vu-Graph board.

Love all, dealer South

Witchdoctor
- ♠ 7 6 4
- ♡ K 8 3
- ◇ A K 7 2
- ♣ 10 5 3

El Saleem
- ♠ K 9
- ♡ 10
- ◇ Q 9 8 3
- ♣ K Q J 8 6 2

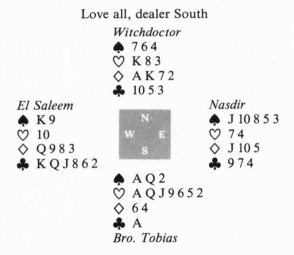

Nasdir
- ♠ J 10 8 5 3
- ♡ 7 4
- ◇ J 10 5
- ♣ 9 7 4

Bro. Tobias
- ♠ A Q 2
- ♡ A Q J 9 6 5 2
- ◇ 6 4
- ♣ A

"A possible slam for North–South," remarked Treacher. "Better than the spade finesse as there are elimination chances."

A shrill whine from the loudspeakers drew a pained expression from the commentator. Why in heaven's name had he agreed to travel so far for such a modest fee? And his room in the hotel was no bigger than a cupboard. "South, of course, is far too strong for a four heart opening," he continued. "The er . . . Upper Bhumpopo team is playing Acol and South's hand fulfils all the requirements for an Acol two bid."

"SOUTH: FOUR HEARTS," came the high-pitched voice of the female announcer from the playing room.

"Four hearts, did she say?" queried Treacher. "Not my choice of opening, I must say. Well, I imagine it will end there. North can hardly advance with both black suits wide open. Just as well, perhaps, with the king of spades offside."

"WEST: FIVE CLUBS."

"Five clubs from West, was that?" said Treacher, peering disapprovingly at the loudspeaker. "An undisciplined call in my opinion. North has a fairly close decision now, whether to double or bid five hearts."

"NORTH: SIX HEARTS."

"Six? Well, evidently North is familiar with his partner's style."

Inside the goldfish bowl there was no further bidding and the chain-smoking El Saleem, the Moroccan captain, led the king of clubs against Brother Tobias's contract of six hearts. When the Witchdoctor put down three small spades followed by three clubs to the ten, Brother Tobias directed a stern expression across the table. This wasn't some 5-beads-a-100 social game; a place in the Bermuda Bowl was at stake. Just as well he had two aces in reserve.

The best chance of avoiding the spade finesse seemed to be to remove West's diamonds and to endplay him with the third round of clubs. There were insufficient entries to ruff both low diamonds as well as a club, but West was unlikely to hold four diamonds, so a partial elimination should suffice. Yes, that should impress old Treacher, thought Brother Tobias.

"Play small," he said, annoyed to see that the Witchdoctor was grinning absurdly at the female announcer and had missed his instruction. "Small!" he reprimanded. "A small club, not a heart."

Brother Tobias won the club lead in hand, crossed to the diamond king and ruffed a club with the 5. He then crossed to the diamond ace and ruffed a low diamond with the jack. The plan now was to take two rounds of trumps, ending in dummy, and to throw West in with the ten of clubs, discarding a spade. Even if West was able to exit safely with a diamond, nothing would be lost. Declarer could still enter dummy with a trump to take the spade finesse.

Brother Tobias reached for the ace of trumps but at the last moment he saw he could improve on his plan if West held the singleton ten of hearts. He pushed back the ace and instead led the queen of hearts from hand. When the ten did appear from West he was able to overtake with dummy's king. The last diamond was ruffed with the ace and dummy entered with the 8 of trumps.

Brother Tobias paused to give Treacher plenty of time to comment on the play. He then called for the ten of clubs. El Saleem was end-played and had to return a spade into declarer's tenace.

Back on the stage Treacher brushed two quarrelsome flies off his sleeve and leaned towards the microphone. "Yes, that was quite well played by er . . . Brother Tobias, a missionary, apparently, who has qualified to play for Upper Bhumpopo after two years with one of the tribes there."

A fat African stood up in the second row of the audience. "Excuse me, sir!" he said. "Dis contract can mos' easily be made by playing ace and one small spade. You see, sir, de king is only once guarded, so . . ."

Treacher interrupted him. "Yes, yes. Declarer could play it that way, of course, but . . ."

The rest of the expert's reply was lost in the ensuing hubbub. Another African, wearing a blue pin-stripe suit, large round glasses, and a bowler hat, obtained silence by rapping his umbrella on the ground. "Old sir," he said. "I am from the Lotengi tribe. My colleagues and I" – he indicated a group who were similarly attired – "consider that North should have been raising four hearts to seven hearts. His partner has shown 8 or 9 playing tricks, he has at least 3, and as you have said in your distinguished workings, playing the hand is often worth one trick. If the spade finesse had been right, there would be many chances to make thirteen tricks with subtle squeezings."

There was some laughter from the back benches. "Thank you for your most valuable contribution," said Treacher. "We have the result from the other table now. South opened two hearts, West overcalled three clubs, and six hearts was soon reached. South won the club lead, drew trumps, and led a diamond to the king. He ruffed a club and ran the trump suit. Then a diamond to the ace reduced everyone to three cards. West came down to ♠ K 9 ♣ Q and was end-played with a club. No swing."

Towards the end of the session there was another slam hand:

N–S game, dealer East

Witchdoctor
♠ 8 7 2
♡ A 8 3
◇ K J 4
♣ 9 8 6 5

El Saleem
♠ 10 9 6 4 3
♡ 9 4
◇ 7 6
♣ J 10 7 3

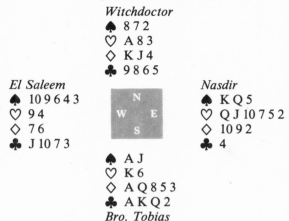

Nasdir
♠ K Q 5
♡ Q J 10 7 5 2
◇ 10 9 2
♣ 4

♠ A J
♡ K 6
◇ A Q 8 5 3
♣ A K Q 2
Bro. Tobias

"EAST: TWO DIAMONDS," came the piercing voice from the loudspeaker.

"That's the Multi again," said Treacher, "usually representing a weak two in one of the majors. Let's see how North–South cope with it."

"SOUTH: THREE NO-TRUMPS."

"Rather a bludgeon of a call. Better to start with a double, I would say."

"WEST: NO BID."

"The learned Doctor has a close decision now," continued Treacher. "Perhaps he's just worth a natural 4 NT."

"NORTH: SIX NO-TRUMPS."

With a mystified expression Treacher turned to the other commentator, a Tunisian in a white djellabah. "Do you know what's going on?" he said. "Was 3 NT conventional in some way?"

"No, I have been watching this pair before. The North player is incurable overbidder, so his partner is always undercooking to compensate."

"Well, it seems South might manage a major-suit squeeze if he escapes a spade lead," said Treacher, speaking into the microphone once more. "Let's see how the play goes."

Back inside the goldfish-bowl El Saleem stubbed out his Turkish cigarette and led the 9 of hearts, expecting this to be his partner's suit.

Brother Tobias won in hand and cashed two club honours, revealing the break. There was a fair chance that East would hold both spade honours along with his announced 6-card heart suit, but it was no use ducking a club now to rectify the count. West would break the squeeze with a second round of hearts.

Instead, Brother Tobias cashed five rounds of diamonds and the queen of clubs. This was the end position when he exited with his last club:

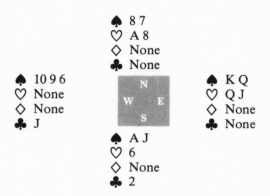

```
              ♠ 8 7
              ♡ A 8
              ◇ None
              ♣ None
 ♠ 10 9 6                    ♠ K Q
 ♡ None        N            ♡ Q J
 ◇ None      W   E          ◇ None
 ♣ J           S            ♣ None
              ♠ A J
              ♡ 6
              ◇ None
              ♣ 2
```

Dummy and East both discarded a spade and Brother Tobias claimed the contract on the spade return.

Back on the commentators' platform, Treacher beckoned unsuccessfully to one of the overworked drinks waiters and resumed his commentary. "Yes, quite unusual to see a forced suicide squeeze at the table," he observed. "Whether the declarer foresaw the ending is another matter."

The last hand looked dull, and Treacher's thoughts wandered to the evening meal in prospect. What was that muck they'd produced last night? Hummus of chick-peas, followed by calves' brains and vegetable marrow? Never again. No, they'd have to find someone else next year – or add a sweetener of a couple of hundred to his fee.

"SOUTH: ONE NO-TRUMP," shrieked the female announcer.

Treacher leaned towards his colleague. "Take over, will you?" he said. "I'm expecting a call from my London paper."

20

Brother Tobias Strikes a Bargain

With two rounds remaining in the African Championship, the Upper Bhumpopo team were lying in third place, 8 VP behind the leaders. Their final match was to be against the powerful Ugandan team, lying second, so it was essential to score well in the afternoon game against the Mauritanian Sahara.

The two ladies were soon in action.

Love all, dealer South

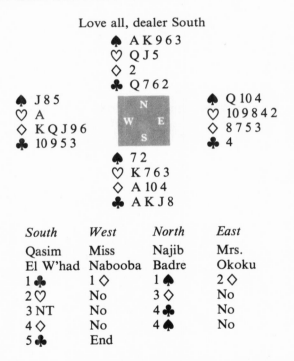

♠ A K 9 6 3
♥ Q J 5
♦ 2
♣ Q 7 6 2

♠ J 8 5   ♠ Q 10 4
♥ A   ♥ 10 9 8 4 2
♦ K Q J 9 6   ♦ 8 7 5 3
♣ 10 9 5 3   ♣ 4

♠ 7 2
♥ K 7 6 3
♦ A 10 4
♣ A K J 8

South	West	North	East
Qasim	Miss	Najib	Mrs.
El W'had	Nabooba	Badre	Okoku
1 ♣	1 ♦	1 ♠	2 ♦
2 ♥	No	3 ♦	No
3 NT	No	4 ♣	No
4 ♦	No	4 ♠	No
5 ♣	End		

The Mauritanian pair, who were clad in blue desert costume, took a good look at the club slam before stopping at the five level. Miss Nabooba led the king of diamonds and the veteran declarer won in hand. He cashed the ace–king of trumps, noting the bad break, and continued with a low heart to West's ace. Miss Nabooba returned

[105]

another high diamond, which was ruffed in dummy. When El W'had called for dummy's queen of hearts, these cards remained:

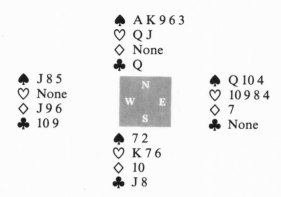

```
                    ♠ A K 9 6 3
                    ♡ Q J
                    ◇ None
                    ♣ Q
    ♠ J 8 5                           ♠ Q 10 4
    ♡ None          N                 ♡ 10 9 8 4
    ◇ J 9 6      W     E              ◇ 7
    ♣ 10 9          S                 ♣ None
                    ♠ 7 2
                    ♡ K 7 6
                    ◇ 10
                    ♣ J 8
```

Miss Nabooba had a count on the hand since her partner, by playing high–low, had signalled an even number of diamonds. It seemed to her that to ruff the queen of hearts and return a diamond would not be good enough. Declarer could then ruff the spades good, draw the last trump and return to dummy with the jack of hearts. She therefore discarded a spade on the heart queen.

El W'had continued with the jack of hearts. Now Miss Nabooba ruffed and forced the dummy again with a third round of diamonds. Declarer could not return to hand without promoting West's remaining trump, so five clubs was one down.

Surely the contract was cold, thought Miss Nabooba. Declarer should have played the queen and ace of trumps, instead of the ace and king. Still, there was no reason to expect a swing. The Witchdoctor was sure to be in six when the board was replayed.

While they were waiting for the other room to finish, the Arab in the South seat lifted an ornate wooden casket on to the table.

"Navud j'hanna al eteni dojdah Sahara," he announced, peering through the slit in his desert headdress.

"He say we have brought many treasures from Sahara," translated the North player. "Maybe you fine ladies would like to buy something."

A succession of glittering objects appeared on the green baize. "This Koran teaching stick is gazelle horn inlaid with silver and copper wire," declared the Arab. "And here is marriage bangle of Bedouh, 200 grammes of fine silver."

"How much de polished amber?" enquired Mrs. Okoku, reaching for her purse.

"Amber bring much good luck," replied the Arab. After a brief colloquy with his superior, he added, "For you he make special price. 200 dirhams."

"Too much," declared Mrs. Okoku. "Half dat price in de souks. Ah! De others have finished."

As Miss Nabooba had feared, the Witchdoctor had gone one off in six on the club hand. The Upper Bhumpopo team was just 7 IMPs ahead with half the boards gone.

For the second half Brother Luke and Mbozi replaced the two ladies. Aggressive bidding by the Witchdoctor resulted in another borderline slam.

N–S game, dealer South

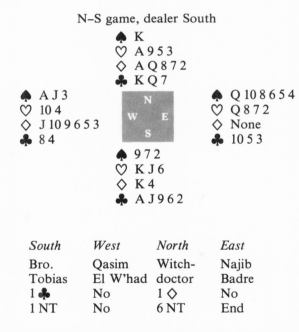

♠ K
♡ A 9 5 3
♦ A Q 8 7 2
♣ K Q 7

♠ A J 3
♡ 10 4
♦ J 10 9 6 5 3
♣ 8 4

♠ Q 10 8 6 5 4
♡ Q 8 7 2
♦ None
♣ 10 5 3

♠ 9 7 2
♡ K J 6
♦ K 4
♣ A J 9 6 2

South	West	North	East
Bro.	Qasim	Witch-	Najib
Tobias	El W'had	doctor	Badre
1 ♣	No	1 ♦	No
1 NT	No	6 NT	End

"N'krah fhemel al bazut s'hen-attot?" enquired the ancient in the West chair, turning towards the Witchdoctor. "Eno Inglezza kufrah 12–16 s'hen-attot fangi, mbele Krowerst timouni."

"He says: how many points the rebid," translated East.

The Witchdoctor gave a loud sniff. "Mos' likely 15–16," he replied.

Brother Tobias glared across the table and pointed a finger at the vulnerability shown on the board.

". . . or mebbe bit less at dis vulnerability," concluded the Witchdoctor. "Only reason I not biddin' seven's cos he can't playin' nothin'," he added in a language that only his opponents could understand.

The jack of diamonds was led, East discarding a spade and declarer winning in hand. A club to the king was followed by the queen of clubs and a successful heart finesse. When the king of hearts was cashed, the ten fell from West and Brother Tobias paused to assess the position.

Hearts seemed to be 2–4, and if East held the ace of spades the contract could be made by reducing the dummy to ♠ K and ♡ A 9. East could then be thrown in with a spade to lead into the heart tenace.

If the spade ace lay with West, the contract could be made in similar fashion. West would have to split his ◇ 10 9, and dummy would be brought down to ♠ K ◇ A 8. West could then be thrown in to give dummy two diamond tricks.

Brother Tobias sighed deeply. How unfair the bridge scoring system was, he thought. The fate of the whole championship might depend on this 50 : 50 guess in a crucial slam contract.

He considered the clues available to him. East was marked with at least six of the outstanding nine spades, so it seemed that the odds were 2 to 1 or better that he held the spade ace. But with six spades to the ace, the queen of hearts and a diamond void, he might well have overcalled. Yes, thought Brother Tobias, and the vulnerability had been in his favour too. Another reason to play West for the spade ace was that the hearts could be tested first, just in case West's ten was a false card.

His mind made up, Brother Tobias led a heart to the ace. West discarded a diamond and declarer now ran his club suit. The fifth club was led to this end position:

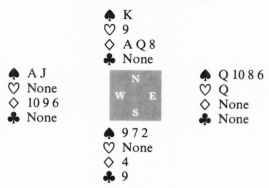

```
                    ♠ K
                    ♡ 9
                    ◇ A Q 8
                    ♣ None
♠ A J                              ♠ Q 10 8 6
♡ None          N                  ♡ Q
◇ 10 9 6     W     E               ◇ None
♣ None          S                  ♣ None
                    ♠ 9 7 2
                    ♡ None
                    ◇ 4
                    ♣ 9
```

West had to discard the jack of spades and dummy threw a heart. After a diamond to the 9 and queen, West was successfully endplayed with the ace of spades.

"The Gods are with us, I think," exclaimed Brother Tobias, mopping his perspiring brow with an outsize handkerchief. "When we're vulnerable the 1 NT rebid is weak, of course."

"Don' matter. You makin' six easy enough," replied the Witch-doctor. "If de rebid was stronger, you mos' probably makin' seven."

When scores were compared at the end of the match, it transpired that the other Mauritanian pair had played the hand in five clubs.

"Hah! Declarer lookin' pretty sick when de dummy went down," said Mbozi. "He think dey missin' cold slam."

"He looked even sicker when we took two diamond ruffs," chortled Brother Luke. "Still, we mustn't laugh. It's rather uncharitable."

The Upper Bhumpopo team had won the match 18–2, putting them within two points of the leaders. Brother Tobias gathered the team round him. "The luck will run our way tonight, never fear," he said. With a flourish he produced a large piece of polished amber from his pocket. "See? I have invested in a good luck charm for us. That shark of an Arab asked 350 dirhams for it . . ." Brother Tobias chuckled ". . . but I wasn't born yesterday. I soon knocked him down to 285."

21

The Magic Card of Bozwambi

With one round to go in the African Championship, the leader board showed:

EGYPT	312
UPPER BHUMPOPO	310
UGANDA	303

Upper Bhumpopo were due to play the Ugandan army team. Egypt also had a difficult match, against unpredictable Zanzibar who were lying fifth.

The final matches were soon under way. An early hand found the Witchdoctor in a no-trump slam.

E–W game, dealer South

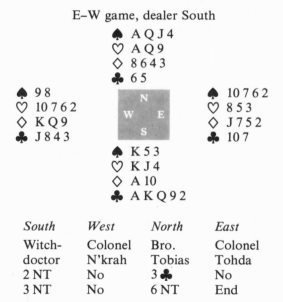

```
                  ♠ A Q J 4
                  ♡ A Q 9
                  ◇ 8 6 4 3
                  ♣ 6 5
   ♠ 9 8                        ♠ 10 7 6 2
   ♡ 10 7 6 2                   ♡ 8 5 3
   ◇ K Q 9                      ◇ J 7 5 2
   ♣ J 8 4 3                    ♣ 10 7
                  ♠ K 5 3
                  ♡ K J 4
                  ◇ A 10
                  ♣ A K Q 9 2
```

South	West	North	East
Witch-	Colonel	Bro.	Colonel
doctor	N'krah	Tobias	Tohda
2 NT	No	3 ♣	No
3 NT	No	6 NT	End

Colonel N'krah, wearing full dress uniform despite the heat, found the one lead to trouble declarer – the king of diamonds. The

Witchdoctor sniffed unpleasantly as the dummy was revealed. Without this diabolical diamond lead he could doubtless have established a twelfth trick in clubs. He won the lead in hand and cashed four spade tricks, discarding a club. Since the bidding marked declarer with a club suit, West retained this suit, discarding two hearts.

Muttering to himself in a strange tongue, the Witchdoctor pressed on with three rounds of hearts. Colonel N'krah fingered a medal thoughtfully. He was unwilling to reduce himself to the queen of diamonds and four clubs to the jack. That would lead to a throw-in at trick eleven if declarer had ♣ A K Q 9 or ♣ A K Q 10 remaining. He therefore discarded the queen of diamonds on declarer's last heart.

The Witchdoctor now cashed two top clubs, his eyes flashing as the ten dropped on his right. This was the end position:

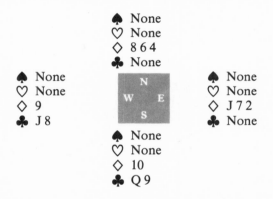

```
              ♠ None
              ♡ None
              ◇ 8 6 4
              ♣ None
  ♠ None                    ♠ None
  ♡ None          N         ♡ None
  ◇ 9        W        E     ◇ J 7 2
  ♣ J 8          S         ♣ None
              ♠ None
              ♡ None
              ◇ 10
              ♣ Q 9
```

All the evidence, particularly West's lengthily-considered discard of the diamond queen, pointed to the clubs being 4–2. The Witchdoctor therefore exited with the ten of diamonds. East saw no future in capturing this card since he would have to give the last two tricks to the dummy. When East played low, the Witchdoctor triumphantly cashed the queen of clubs for the contract.

"Hah! Six o' diamonds Bozwambi magic card," he exclaimed. "I knew we makin' de slam when I seein' him in de dummy."

"What an absurd superstition," declared Brother Tobias, chuckling to himself as he fingered the lucky piece of amber in his pocket. "How can a playing card have magic powers?"

When the hand was replayed, North was declarer in six no-trumps and scored an easy twelve tricks after a heart lead. The half-time comparison put the Upper Bhumpopo team just 5 IMPs in the lead.

Neither side had made much headway when the very last hand of the whole championship found Brother Tobias in four hearts.

Game all, dealer South

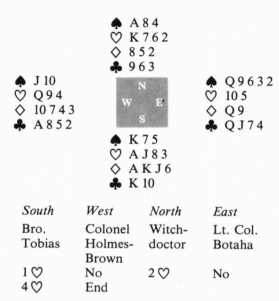

```
              ♠ A 8 4
              ♡ K 7 6 2
              ◇ 8 5 2
              ♣ 9 6 3
♠ J 10                          ♠ Q 9 6 3 2
♡ Q 9 4            N            ♡ 10 5
◇ 10 7 4 3     W      E         ◇ Q 9
♣ A 8 5 2         S             ♣ Q J 7 4
              ♠ K 7 5
              ♡ A J 8 3
              ◇ A K J 6
              ♣ K 10
```

South	West	North	East
Bro.	Colonel	Witch-	Lt. Col.
Tobias	Holmes-	doctor	Botaha
	Brown		
1 ♡	No	2 ♡	No
4 ♡	End		

The jet-black African sitting West, who by some quirk of history was called Holmes-Brown, selected the jack of spades as his opening lead. Brother Tobias won in dummy and finessed the jack of diamonds successfully. He then crossed to the king of trumps and finessed the jack of trumps, less successfully. When West returned the ten of spades, declarer won in hand and drew the last trump.

Brother Tobias now tested the diamond suit, hoping to discard dummy's spade loser. When they failed to divide, his last effort was to cross to dummy with a diamond ruff and lead towards the king of clubs. Colonel Holmes-Brown won with the ace and Brother Tobias conceded one down.

"Two finesses wrong and the diamonds not breaking," he said, writing down the score with a resigned air. "I held your magic card, too, so that rather disproves your theory."

The Witchdoctor shrugged his shoulders. "Bwana not even tryin' to make magic. If you throwin' de spade on de magic card, you makin' if West have doubleton spade. He endplayed."

Brother Tobias reached feverishly for West's cards and thumbed through them. Only two spades could be found. "Good God, I could have made it!" he exclaimed. "If that costs us the championship, I'll never forgive myself."

Mbozi and Brother Luke soon appeared. They had made little impression in the other room and the Upper Bhumpopo team found that they had lost the match by 13 VPs to 7. They were still 1 VP ahead of Uganda, but Egypt were almost certain to win.

"UGANDA 13, UPPER BHUMPOPO 7," came a shrill voice from the loudspeaker.

"As if we didn't know," muttered Brother Tobias. "Fancy paying 285 dirhams for this lucky piece of amber. It must have had a curse on it."

"We still in with chance, Bwana," said Miss Nabooba, who had just returned from a scouting trip to find out the other scores. "Egypt losin' at half-time."

"ZANZIBAR 14, EGYPT 6," came the news from the loud-speaker. "Egypt win the championship by just 1 VP from Upper Bhumpopo!"

Brother Tobias slumped back in his chair. His misplay on the last hand had cost them a place in the Bermuda Bowl.

The crowd of players milled forward to the stage where the Tunisian Minister of Culture was waiting to present the trophy.

"Attention! Attention!" announced the loudspeaker. "We have corrected result: ZANZIBAR 19, EGYPT 1."

"Hah! Egypt only gettin' pathetic 1 point, Bwana," exclaimed Mbozi. "We's done it!"

Brother Tobias raised his eyes heavenwards. His prayers had been answered. Or could that piece of amber possibly have . . .

The Minister of Culture reached for the ornate silver cup and Brother Tobias walked proudly forward to receive it.

"Zanzibar now win the championship on a split tie with Upper Bhumpopo!" declared the loudspeaker. "Ah, there's the winning captain. All be applauding, please!"

PART III

Return to the Monastery

22

Brother Aelred's Contribution

On the second Tuesday of every month the monastery duplicate
evening took the form of a random teams event with each pair
drawing for teammates.

"Shall I pick a number for us, Abbot?" said Brother Lucius
breezily.

"Leave it to me," said the Abbot, marching towards the polished
oak table. "This is important." He stood still for a moment, raising
his eyes to heaven, then selected one of the five remaining balls of
paper.

"What team number have you picked, Abbot?" asked Brother
Xavier, who was organising the event as usual.

"Seven," replied the Abbot grimly.

"Oh, that's a remarkably lucky draw," declared Brother Xavier,
looking at the team sheet.

"You see, Lucius?" said the Abbot triumphantly.

"Sorry, I didn't mean it was lucky for you, Abbot," replied Brother
Xavier. "I meant it was lucky for Brother Aelred and Brother
Michael."

One hand early in the evening gave the Abbot a chance to shine in
defence.

East–West game, dealer South

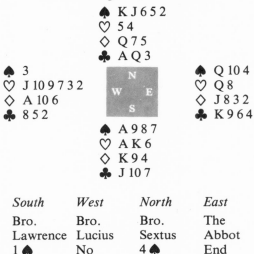

```
              ♠ K J 6 5 2
              ♡ 5 4
              ◇ Q 7 5
              ♣ A Q 3
♠ 3                           ♠ Q 10 4
♡ J 10 9 7 3 2                ♡ Q 8
◇ A 10 6                      ◇ J 8 3 2
♣ 8 5 2                       ♣ K 9 6 4
              ♠ A 9 8 7
              ♡ A K 6
              ◇ K 9 4
              ♣ J 10 7
```

South	*West*	*North*	*East*
Bro.	Bro.	Bro.	The
Lawrence	Lucius	Sextus	Abbot
1 ♠	No	4 ♠	End

For his opening lead Brother Lucius looked no further than the jack of hearts, captured in hand by the black-bearded Brother Lawrence. If the club king was onside declarer could permit himself the luxury of a trump safety play (low to the king on the first round), so his first move was an exploratory club to the queen. When the Abbot won the king and fired back the queen of hearts, declarer won and played the A K of trumps, disclosing the adverse break.

Reading the hand well, he proceeded to cash out the clubs before taking his heart ruff. The Abbot declined to overruff but was thrown in with a trump at the next trick and therefore had to open the diamond suit.

With a knowledgeable air he advanced the jack of diamonds. Placing the Abbot with J 10, Brother Lawrence ran the trick to dummy's queen and surrendered the next two diamond tricks to go one down.

"By the play of a single card," declared the Abbot dramatically, "I have demonstrated the enormous gulf that lies between expert and non-expert. Had I led a low diamond, Brother Lawrence, you could scarcely have gone wrong."

"Had you led the 8 of diamonds he couldn't possibly have gone right," observed Brother Lucius as they moved for the next round. "On the lead of the jack he might have applied the Principle of

Restricted Choice and played you for a single honour rather than J 10."

The Abbot defended himself well. "Ah, but there is a psychological point here," he replied. "Brother Lawrence wouldn't know the Principle of Restricted Choice from Albanian black pudding. No, I was confident he would misread the jack and such failure is very dispiriting for the opposition."

"Do you mean," enquired Brother Lucius, "that he would lose heart and concede swings in the remaining matches? That doesn't help us."

Ignoring this, the Abbot studied his score-card. "Three rounds to go, and only about 40 IMPs up?" he exclaimed. "That's no good with Brother Aelred in support. We must stir ourselves."

The next few rounds produced little action, and when the final board of the evening arrived the Abbot had a determined glint in his eye.

N–S game, dealer South

```
                    ♠ 6 5
                    ♡ K J 9
                    ◇ A J 6
                    ♣ A Q 9 6 2
  ♠ J 8                              ♠ K 10 9 4 3
  ♡ 10 7 6 2          N             ♡ Q 3
  ◇ K 10 8 7 4 3   W     E          ◇ Q 5 2
  ♣ 7                 S             ♣ J 4 3
                    ♠ A Q 7 2
                    ♡ A 8 5 4
                    ◇ 9
                    ♣ K 10 8 5
```

South	West	North	East
The	Bro.	Bro.	Bro.
Abbot	Xavier	Lucius	Paulo
1♣	No	1◇	No
1♡	No	1♠	No
2♠	No	4♣	No
6♣	End		

Like a rocket destined for the moon, the auction lifted off slowly, then accelerated into the stratosphere. The Abbot stretched to the limit with his final call, hoping to generate a swing on the hand.

West led a diamond and the Abbot was surprised to find that the slam was a sound venture after all. Two diamond ruffs in hand would bring the total to eleven tricks and there were excellent chances of a twelfth trick in the major suits.

Winning the diamond lead in dummy, he ruffed a diamond and crossed to the ace of trumps. Next he ruffed dummy's last diamond and cashed the king of trumps, West discarding a diamond.

"Now we come to the main business of the hand," said the Abbot, leading a low heart. "Try the jack will you?"

The finesse lost and Brother Paulo returned a low spade. The Abbot now had to make his play in spades before he could test the heart suit. Even if East did hold the spade king, the finesse would be necessary only if he also held a doubleton heart. If he held three hearts the suit would break; and if he held more than three hearts the trick lost by spurning the finesse would return on a major-suit squeeze. The Abbot therefore won the trick with the ace of spades. He crossed to the heart king and ran dummy's trumps but none of his chances materialised. West won the last heart trick to put the contract one down.

"Not our evening, I fear," said the Abbot. "To finesse in spades would be a clear mistake."

Brother Lucius entered the score on his card but said nothing.

"Can you not run the jack of hearts to West?" suggested Brother Paulo. "Even if it is losing, you can test the hearts before falling back to the spade finesse."

"That's true, Abbot," said Brother Xavier. "And if East covers, of course, the 9–8 are equals against the ten."

"Two-way finesses are always easier in the post-mortem," retorted the Abbot, rising to his feet. "The board will be flat, I dare say."

"That is most unlikely, I think," said Brother Paulo, smiling at his partner. "In fact it is rather looking as if the board will be passed out."

The Abbot stared at Brother Paulo. Had overwork or exposure to the English climate affected his brain?

"Our other pair are Brother Godfrey and Brother Julius of the silent Eustacian order," continued Brother Paulo, "so presumably they will be passing throughout the evening."

"Look, if I'd known that, I would have stopped in five clubs and chalked up a certain 12 IMPs," declared the Abbot. "Surely if your other pair are Eustacians it should be written on your convention card." The Abbot thumped the table. "Director!" he called.

The ancient Brother Zac appeared on the scene and consulted the index of his rule-book. "This is one of the most interesting queries I have ever encountered," he observed. "Let's see . . . there's nothing given under 'E' for Eustacian. Ah, what have we here? *Silent bidders, use of.* No, that's not what we want, is it? I think I may say, Abbot, with reasonable certitude, that the Laws do not envisage such a situation. First thing tomorrow I'll draft a letter to . . ."

"I see our illustrious teammates have finished," interrupted the Abbot. "Time to hear the worst, Lucius. Let's go!"

"We've had a few bad ones," Brother Aelred confided excitedly, "but we've one enormous board to make up for it. You know that cold club slam? Well, I opened with an incredibly daring three diamond bid on the West cards."

"Yes," said Brother Michael. "And when I raised to five diamonds, pretending I had a good hand, nobody even doubled! Just 250 away."

"You went to the five level to silence opponents who haven't said a word for twenty years?" cried the Abbot. "Didn't you realise you were playing a Eustacian pair? Didn't it occur to you to look at their convention card?"

"Well, yes of course I did," replied Brother Aelred. "But, you see, it was completely empty. They hadn't filled it in at all."

23

The Mystery of Friar Fawcett

Brother Sextus, the monastery janitor, had just finished the Church News crossword when there was a loud knock on the monastery outer door. Who could it be so late at night, he wondered, as he crossed the cobbled courtyard. He swung back the heavy oak door to reveal an elderly friar in a black cassock.

"Can you shelter me for the night, Brother?" said the friar. "I am weary from long travel."

"You are most welcome," replied Brother Sextus. "Come this way."

It transpired that the friar was an occasional bridge player and the monks soon inveigled him into a £1 game, hoping to exact some payment for his night's lodging.

N–S game, dealer South

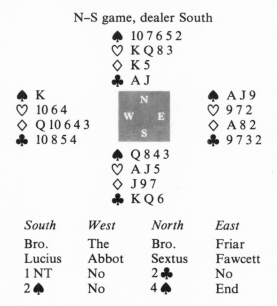

```
              ♠ 10 7 6 5 2
              ♡ K Q 8 3
              ◇ K 5
              ♣ A J
♠ K                           ♠ A J 9
♡ 10 6 4                      ♡ 9 7 2
◇ Q 10 6 4 3                  ◇ A 8 2
♣ 10 8 5 4                    ♣ 9 7 3 2
              ♠ Q 8 4 3
              ♡ A J 5
              ◇ J 9 7
              ♣ K Q 6
```

South	West	North	East
Bro.	The	Bro.	Friar
Lucius	Abbot	Sextus	Fawcett
1 NT	No	2 ♣	No
2 ♠	No	4 ♠	End

The Abbot, who had suffered the misfortune to cut the friar as partner, led the four of diamonds against the spade game. Brother Lucius played low from dummy and East won with the ace.

"Only two clubs in the dummy?" queried the friar. "I thought you bid clubs."

"Yes, but that was the Stayman convention," replied Brother Sextus. "Surely you've heard of it? It asks the opener to show a four-card major."

"What a clever idea," said the friar, making a note of the convention on a scrap of paper. "It's amazing the things they dream up nowadays."

The friar's diamond return was taken in the dummy and a small trump was led. The friar played the jack, Brother Lucius covered with the queen and the Abbot's bare king won the trick. Two further trump tricks had to be lost and the contract was one down.

"That was a funny play, your jack of spades," said Brother Lucius, giving the friar a puzzled look. "If you'd played the nine, I would have taken the percentage play of ducking in hand and made the contract."

"So you would," said the Abbot, smiling at the turn of events. "It was a curious play, certainly, but it worked out well."

"Yes," said the friar with a blank expression. "I thought I'd better play the jack to try and force out an honour."

Brother Lucius reached stoically for his scorepad and the play proceeded.

Although the friar appeared by his comments to be a novice, he could seemingly do nothing wrong at the table. When the monastery clock tower sounded midnight, after which no new rubbers were allowed to start, he had accumulated some £50. This was the second hand of the final rubber.

Love all, dealer South

              ♠ 8
              ♡ A K Q 4
              ◇ Q 6
              ♣ A Q J 9 7 2

♠ A 9 2   ♠ 10 5
♡ 10 8 2   ♡ J 9 6 3
◇ A K 10 8 7 5   ◇ J 3 2
♣ 8   ♣ K 10 6 4

              ♠ K Q J 7 6 4 3
              ♡ 7 5
              ◇ 9 4
              ♣ 5 3

The Mystery of Friar Fawcett

South	West	North	East
Bro.	Friar	Bro.	The
Sextus	Fawcett	Lucius	Abbot
3♠	No	4♠	End

The friar, now holding the West cards, led out the top two diamonds against four spades. The Abbot indicated an odd number of cards in the suit by signalling with the two and the three. The friar continued with another diamond and looked disappointed when the Abbot followed with the jack. "I'm so sorry, partner," he said. "I thought you might be able to overruff the dummy."

"With a doubleton diamond it might just have occurred to me to give you a high-low signal," replied the Abbot.

"Quite so," said the friar. "When I saw your three on the second round, I naturally assumed that your first card had been a higher one."

Declarer ruffed the third round of diamonds in hand and led the jack of trumps. Friar Fawcett jumped in with the ace, scratched his head for a couple of seconds and then led a fourth round of diamonds. The Abbot, sitting East, ruffed with the ten of spades, blasting a hole in declarer's trump holding. The friar's nine of trumps became the setting trick.

"Thank heavens you misread my signal in diamonds," exclaimed the Abbot. "What a stroke of luck!"

"There was no need for such a fancy defence," declared Brother Sextus. "If the friar switches to a club or heart at trick three, he can lock me in dummy when he wins with the ace of spades."

"No, not necessarily," pointed out Brother Lucius. "After a switch you could cash the ace of clubs and the ace–king–queen of hearts, throwing a club from hand. Now when the friar won the ace of trumps he'd have to give you an entry to hand."

The following day the mysterious friar breakfasted early and bade a hasty farewell to the monastery.

"He was an odd fellow, that friar," said the Abbot later that morning. "In fact I don't believe he was a friar at all. I wonder if he could be an impostor from one of the London card clubs?"

"You could be right, Abbot," replied Brother Sextus. "I certainly haven't heard of the order that he belonged to."

"What order? He never mentioned it, did he?"

"No, but I spotted it on the label inside the back of his cassock," replied Brother Sextus. "It was some strange community called Moss Brothers."

[121]

24

The Penance of Brother Julius

With the air of a Roman emperor entering the senate, the Abbot made his way into the main cardroom. He turned to address his partner, Brother Lucius. "The first round often sets the pattern for the evening," he remarked. "We can do no better than start at Brother Aelred's table."

"These seats are free, I take it," said the Abbot, easing himself into the East chair and noting it was none too comfortable.

"Well, er . . . yes," replied Brother Aelred, "but we usually begin against Brother Zac and Brother Edwin."

"So that one side or other must get off to a good start," explained Brother Michael.

The Abbot was not listening. "Some of these chairs are in a disgraceful state," he observed, trying to prod the upholstery into shape. "I told Brother Julius to see to them over two weeks ago. Remind me to bring up the subject when we play against him."

The first round was soon under way.

Game all, dealer South

♠ K Q 8 7 3
♡ A Q J 4
◇ 6 4 3
♣ 6

♠ 10 5 2   ♠ A J 9 4
♡ 7 5 3   ♡ K 8 2
◇ 10 8 2   ◇ 9
♣ Q 10 8 3   ♣ 9 7 5 4 2

♠ 6
♡ 10 9 6
◇ A K Q J 7 5
♣ A K J

South	West	North	East
Bro.	Bro.	Bro.	The
Aelred	Lucius	Michael	Abbot
2 ◇	No	2 ♠	No
3 ◇	No	3 ♡	No
4 NT	No	5 ◇	No
6 ◇	No	No	No

Brother Lucius led a low club against six diamonds and Brother Aelred won in hand with the jack. The contract seemed to depend on the heart finesse. But after the club lead, didn't he have a second chance? Yes! He could lead a spade towards dummy, hoping that West had the ace. If West went in with the ace, there would be two discards for the heart losers. And if West didn't play the ace, declarer wouldn't lose a spade and could finesse in hearts for the overtrick.

Brother Aelred sat back in his chair, somewhat exhausted by this analysis. Then, putting his plan into action, he drew three rounds of trumps and led a spade to the king. The Abbot won with the ace and returned a club. Brother Aelred now had to resort to the heart finesse. When it failed, he was one down.

"Can't be helped, partner," said Brother Michael. "One of two finesses. We had to be in it."

"It's not one of two on a heart lead," replied Brother Aelred. "You gave me a second chance, there, Lucius."

"Yes, he also gave you a third chance," remarked the Abbot. "Spades were 4–3. If you ruff the ace and king of clubs, you've enough entries to set up the spade suit."

Brother Lucius nodded his agreement. "You can't afford to draw any trumps on that line, though," he said. "You must play a spade at trick 2."

"Is that right?" queried Brother Aelred. "You might go in with the ace of spades and switch to a heart through the ace–queen. I have to put up the ace and now the top spades might get ruffed."

"Yes, but you don't have to play the spade honours immediately," explained Brother Lucius. "You can pull two rounds of trumps and return to dummy with a club ruff."

Brother Aelred shook his head, unconvinced. "I still think it pays to draw trumps first in the long run," he said.

The next board was soon on the table.

E–W game, dealer West

```
              ♠ None
              ♡ A K
              ◇ J 8 6 3
              ♣ A K 9 8 6 5 2
  ♠ 7 6 4                      ♠ Q J 10 9 2
  ♡ 8 6 3          N          ♡ 9 4 2
  ◇ A 9 7 2     W     E       ◇ K Q 10
  ♣ Q 10 3         S          ♣ 7 4
              ♠ A K 8 5 3
              ♡ Q J 10 7 5
              ◇ 5 4
              ♣ J
```

South	West	North	East
Bro.	Bro.	Bro.	The
Aelred	Lucius	Michael	Abbot
	No	1 ♣	No
1 ♡	No	2 ◇	No
2 ♠	No	3 ♣	No
3 NT	No	No	No

After a maladjusted auction to 3 NT, Brother Lucius led the two of diamonds and the Abbot won with the ten. He cashed the other two diamond winners and paused to assess the position. If the clubs were solid, declarer had nine tricks ready to run. A spade switch would therefore be essential. Now, what if Lucius had a club stop? No problem there, thought the Abbot. Lucius would be able to cash the ace of diamonds when declarer cleared the club suit. Seeing no more to the position, the Abbot switched to the queen of spades.

Brother Aelred won with the ace and discarded dummy's ace of hearts. He found advanced plays like this very easy; they were in the magazines every week. It was straightforward hands that he tended to misplay. He continued with the king of spades, throwing dummy's other heart honour. He now cashed five rounds of hearts, the last of which squeezed Brother Lucius in the minors. Giving a look of puzzlement when the ace of diamonds was discarded, Brother Aelred claimed ten tricks.

"Yes, at double-dummy I can break it by returning a heart," remarked the Abbot. He gave a short laugh. "You wouldn't thank me if you held the ace of spades, though, and declarer's clubs were solid."

"True," replied Brother Lucius. "But if I held the spade ace, I suppose I should play ◇ 9 on the second round, followed by ◇ 7, a McKenney signal."

The last hand of the first round was soon dealt:

Love all, dealer North

Bro. Michael
♠ 10 6 2
♡ Q 10 8 7 3
◇ 4
♣ Q 10 7 4

Bro. Lucius
♠ K 8 4
♡ K 4
◇ 9 8 6 2
♣ A K J 6

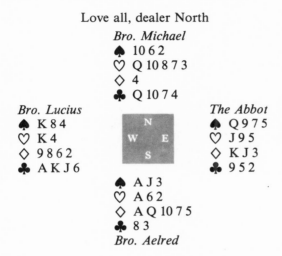

The Abbot
♠ Q 9 7 5
♡ J 9 5
◇ K J 3
♣ 9 5 2

♠ A J 3
♡ A 6 2
◇ A Q 10 7 5
♣ 8 3
Bro. Aelred

"One diamond," said Brother Aelred, sitting South.

Too weak in the majors for a takeout double, Brother Lucius passed and Brother Michael responded one heart. Brother Aelred paused to consider his rebid. Since North had changed the suit, rather than make a weakness takeout of 1 NT, he should have at least nine points. Fifteen and nine was . . . yes, twenty-four. Enough for a game try. "Two no-trumps," said Brother Aelred.

Brother Michael, who had ample experience of Brother Aelred's skill at no-trump contracts, decided to look for a safer spot. "Three clubs," he said.

Three hearts was the obvious bid now, but as his partner was not renowned for his play in suit contracts, Brother Aelred settled for 3 NT. This had been the auction:

South	West	North	East
Bro.	Bro.	Bro.	The
Aelred	Lucius	Michael	Abbot
		No	No
1 ◇	No	1 ♡	No
2 NT	No	3 ♣	No
3 NT	End		

Brother Lucius led the four of spades to the two, nine and jack. Brother Aelred inspected dummy's meagre resources, muttering something under his breath. Ace and another heart put Brother Lucius on lead, and he played back the king of spades. Brother Aelred ducked this trick and won the spade continuation. He now ran the heart suit. The last heart was led to this end position:

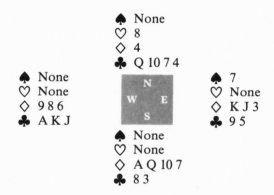

```
                    ♠ None
                    ♡ 8
                    ◇ 4
                    ♣ Q 10 7 4
  ♠ None                          ♠ 7
  ♡ None           N              ♡ None
  ◇ 9 8 6      W       E          ◇ K J 3
  ♣ A K J          S              ♣ 9 5
                    ♠ None
                    ♡ None
                    ◇ A Q 10 7
                    ♣ 8 3
```

All three players discarded a club and Brother Aelred continued with a diamond to the ten. When this held the trick, he exited in clubs, hoping for the best. At trick 12 Brother Lucius had to return a diamond into the ace–queen, giving declarer nine tricks and the contract.

"How many off?" enquired Brother Michael, reaching for the score sheet.

"Made on the nose," replied Brother Aelred resentfully. "Weren't you watching?"

The Abbot entered the score on his card and returned his attention to the upholstery of his chair. "Sitting in this chair for an evening would be a category-2 penance in itself," he remarked. "In fact, that's not such a bad idea in the circumstances. We meet Brother Julius on the next round, I see."

25

The Abbot and the Cake Knife

The Abbot entered the darkened infirmary and approached the bed where Brother Xavier was lying.

"Are you awake?" he bellowed.

Brother Xavier woke with a start and raised himself on one elbow. "Oh, hullo, Abbot. Kind of you to pay me a visit."

"I didn't climb forty-five steps just to pass the time of day," declared the Abbot, pausing to regain his breath. "I want to know if you'll be fit for this afternoon's Crockford's match."

"I'd hate to let the monastery down, Abbot," replied Brother Xavier, "but my temperature touched 104 yesterday and I have a headache I wouldn't wish on my worst enemy."

"Well, I've often played with a headache," observed the Abbot. "It just requires a little extra concentration, that's all."

"What if my condition is infectious, Abbot?"

"Infectious?" said the Abbot, retreating from the bedside. "Very well, I'll ask Brother Sextus to stand in for you."

"I'm not sure he's eligible," replied Brother Xavier. "Wasn't he in the monastery second team that played in the Maidenhead heat?"

"One monk looks much like another," said the Abbot. "Brother Sextus will know where his duties lie."

That afternoon the monastery team arrived punctually at the venue for their match, a thatched vicarage in Aylesbury. Their opponents were the vicar's wife and three members of her husband's church. Brother Sextus was soon in action.

N–S game, dealer South

```
                    ♠ K 10 9
                    ♡ K Q 9
                    ◇ A J 9 4
                    ♣ J 7 3
    ♠ Q J 7 6 3        ┌─────┐        ♠ A 8 5 4 2
    ♡ 7 4              │  N  │        ♡ A 10 6 5 2
    ◇ 8 3              │ W E │        ◇ K 6 5
    ♣ 8 5 4 2          │  S  │        ♣ None
                       └─────┘
                    ♠ None
                    ♡ J 8 3
                    ◇ Q 10 7 2
                    ♣ A K Q 10 9 6
```

South	*West*	*North*	*East*
Bro.	Mrs.	The	Mrs.
Sextus	Wicket	Abbot	Godfrey
1 ♣	1 ♠	3 NT	4 ♠
5 ♣	End		

Mrs. Wicket led the queen of spades against five clubs. Brother Sextus covered with dummy's king and ruffed when East's ace appeared. It seemed that six clubs would have depended only on the diamond finesse, but a round of trumps disclosed the 4–0 break, putting even five clubs at risk.

Brother Sextus drew trumps in four rounds, leaving himself with just one trump, then turned his attention to the red suits. Since a spade lead from East would be disastrous, he decided to play first on hearts, the suit of West's potential entry. East won the ace of hearts and returned a spade, but Brother Sextus was not unduly concerned. West was clearly marked with the king of diamonds to make up her overcall. He ruffed the spade return and ran the queen of diamonds.

"Oh dear, I'm sorry about this," said Mrs. Godfrey, as she sheepishly produced the king of diamonds and the defenders cashed three spade tricks. "That was very bad luck. 300 to us, is it?"

Brother Sextus blinked. "Yes," he said. "Still, it was a good sacrifice against four spades."

"It would have been an even better sacrifice if you'd thought for a moment at trick one," remarked the Abbot. "If you play low on the spade lead, neither defender can subsequently attack the suit. Five clubs is easily made."

"You were a bit light there, weren't you, Adelaine?" said Mrs. Godfrey.

"Well, I wanted to take up their bidding space," replied her partner. "I don't like to pass with a five-timer, anyway."

"Didn't we play against you in the qualifier at Maidenhead?" asked Mrs. Godfrey, turning once more to Brother Sextus. "You were playing with a different partner, weren't you? You had a misunderstanding over Aspro, I seem to remember."

"You must be mistaken, Madam," intervened the Abbot. "We qualified at the Bristol heat, and my partner has a faultless knowledge of the Aspro convention, I assure you."

Scores were level at the first change. A hand late in the second set saw the vicar's wife, a life master and captain of the team, at the helm in an awkward slam contract.

E–W game, dealer South

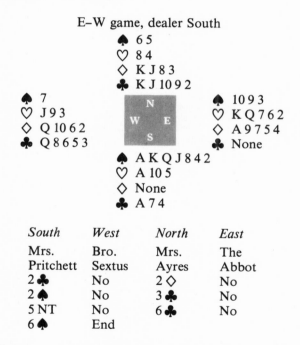

	♠ 6 5	
	♡ 8 4	
	◇ K J 8 3	
	♣ K J 10 9 2	

♠ 7   ♠ 10 9 3
♡ J 9 3   ♡ K Q 7 6 2
◇ Q 10 6 2   ◇ A 9 7 5 4
♣ Q 8 6 5 3   ♣ None

♠ A K Q J 8 4 2
♡ A 10 5
◇ None
♣ A 7 4

South	West	North	East
Mrs.	Bro.	Mrs.	The
Pritchett	Sextus	Ayres	Abbot
2♣	No	2◇	No
2♠	No	3♣	No
5 NT	No	6♣	No
6♠	End		

When Mrs. Pritchett heard of a club suit opposite, she made an immediate Grand Slam Force of five no-trumps. The stockily-built Mrs. Ayres denied two of the top three honours, so Mrs. Pritchett subsided in six spades.

Brother Sextus was disappointed to hear this correction into spades, but took consolation from the fact that his partner might well be void in clubs. "My lead, is it?" he said, detaching the five of clubs.

The Abbot ruffed, as expected, and Mrs. Pritchett unblocked the ace of clubs from hand. With dummy's proven tenace sitting over West's queen, the ace could serve no purpose. Retaining two low clubs in hand would allow an extra entry to dummy.

The Abbot paused briefly to consider his return. Should he try to cash the ace of diamonds? No, declarer's 5 NT bid was surely based on solid spades, a club fit and first-round controls in the red suits. Instead he returned the king of hearts, won by declarer's ace.

Mrs. Pritchett adjusted her gold-rimmed spectacles. She could count eleven tricks, and a minor-suit squeeze would succeed if West held the ace of diamonds. However, the Abbot's pause before making the obvious switch to hearts rather suggested that he held the diamond ace. Playing on that assumption, Mrs. Pritchett drew trumps and entered dummy with a club finesse, taking advantage of her earlier unblock in the suit. She now led the king of diamonds, hoping to transfer the diamond guard to West, the hand who would also have to guard the clubs. The Abbot, to his credit, had read the position and followed smoothly with a low diamond.

Mrs. Pritchett fingered her pearls undecidedly. She was not committed to running the king; she could ruff and play West for both the missing honours. Eventually, though, she played on her earlier hunch, discarding a heart from hand and claiming the contract when West followed helplessly with a small diamond.

Mrs. Pritchett smiled at the Abbot, acknowledging his fine defensive effort. "And now please excuse me," she said. "I must put on the kettle for tea."

Brother Sextus sighed as he returned his cards to the wallet. "I'm afraid she made rather a fool of us there, Abbot," he said.

"What do you mean?" said the Abbot sharply.

"Well, you know, slipping that king of diamonds through," replied Brother Sextus. "Still, I suppose it was difficult for you."

The Abbot glared blackly across the table. "I shall be bringing out several instructive points from this hand at my next intermediate class," he said. "I trust you will find it convenient to attend."

At the tea interval the monastery team was 22 IMPs adrift. Their spirits were revived by the splendid sight of the vicarage tea-table, heavily laden with scones, fish-paste sandwiches, buttered muffins, shrimps, winkles and an outsize chocolate cake.

"What a delight to the eye!" exclaimed the Abbot. "I haven't tasted winkles since my childhood. And do I spy a chocolate cake?"

"Yes," beamed Mrs. Wicket. "I made that. I hope you like it; it has rum in the recipe."

"And now, Abbot," said the vicar's wife. "Perhaps you would do the honours?"

"Yes, indeed," replied the Abbot, reaching for the cake knife.

Mrs. Pritchett was much amused. "What a wicked sense of humour, Abbot," she said. "No, what I meant, of course, was the grace. Would you be so kind?"

The tea was soon in full swing. Mrs. Wicket, clutching her tea cup, edged her way nervously towards the Abbot. "I'm so glad you like the chocolate cake," she said. "I was worried it might be against regulations, having rum in it."

"We are a strict order at St. Titus, it is true," declared the Abbot, pausing to cut himself another slice. "But some flexibility is called for, I think. Particularly when you've gone to so much trouble."

The Abbot was eventually prised from the tea-table, and the match resumed.

N–S game, dealer North

```
           ♠ 9 5 3
           ♡ 10 8 4
           ◇ A K 4
           ♣ A K Q 5
♠ K Q 10 8 7 6 2        ♠ J 4
♡ J                     ♡ K 9 6 3
◇ Q 10 7 3              ◇ J 6 5 2
♣ 8                     ♣ 9 4 3
           ♠ A
           ♡ A Q 7 5 2
           ◇ 9 8
           ♣ J 10 7 6 2
```

South	West	North	East
The Abbot	Mrs. Wicket	Bro. Sextus	Mrs. Godfrey
		1 NT	No
3 ♡	3 ♠	4 ♡	No
4 NT	No	5 ♡	No
6 ♡	No	No	No

With a fit already found in hearts, the Abbot saw no purpose in informing the defenders of his club suit. After checking on aces he bid six hearts, confident from the spade overcall that partner would not have wasted values in that suit.

Mrs. Wicket led the king of spades to South's ace, and the Abbot saw that the play of the hand would turn on the trump suit. His first move was to cash the ace of trumps, dropping West's jack. Next he crossed to a diamond honour and led the ten of trumps. Mrs. Godfrey went in with the king and forced declarer with a second round of spades. The Abbot crossed to dummy's remaining diamond honour and surveyed this end-position:

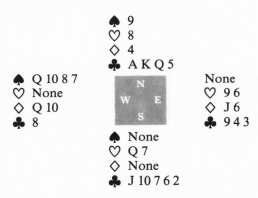

It was apparent that he should have unblocked the eight on the first round of trumps; he could then have finessed the seven at this stage and claimed the contract. With a resigned air he called for the eight of trumps but Mrs. Godfrey played low, refusing to assist him. Now if he crossed to the jack of clubs to draw the last trump the club suit would be blocked and dummy would have to surrender the last trick. There was only one chance and the Abbot steeled himself to take it.

"Ace of clubs," he said, letting Brother Sextus know from his expression that the contract was now at the crossroads, ". . . and the king, please."

When West showed out on this card, the Abbot crossed triumphantly to the jack of clubs and drew the last trump, discarding dummy's queen of clubs. With a flourish he displayed his two good clubs and claimed the contract.

"Couldn't you have unblocked that eight of trumps, Abbot?" said Brother Sextus.

"The odd sword stroke will always go astray in the heat of battle," replied the Abbot, well pleased with himself.

The teams had just finished scoring the third set when the vicar, Mr. Pritchett, returned from the evening service. "What's this, Gloria?" he said, poking his head into the room. "Not conceded the match yet?"

"Not with a margin of just 15 IMPs," replied his wife tartly. "Particularly as it's in our favour."

"Wonders will never cease," said the vicar. "May I help myself to a slice of Mrs. Wicket's chocolate cake? I was thinking about it all through the last hymn."

"I'm afraid that proved rather popular," replied his wife. "There are one or two fish-paste sandwiches left, I think."

The last set was keenly fought. This was the penultimate board:

E–W game, dealer North

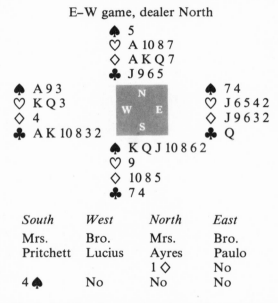

```
                  ♠ 5
                  ♡ A 10 8 7
                  ◇ A K Q 7
                  ♣ J 9 6 5
  ♠ A 9 3                        ♠ 7 4
  ♡ K Q 3                        ♡ J 6 5 4 2
  ◇ 4                            ◇ J 9 6 3 2
  ♣ A K 10 8 3 2                 ♣ Q
                  ♠ K Q J 10 8 6 2
                  ♡ 9
                  ◇ 10 8 5
                  ♣ 7 4
```

South	West	North	East
Mrs.	Bro.	Mrs.	Bro.
Pritchett	Lucius	Ayres	Paulo
		1 ◇	No
4 ♠	No	No	No

The stockily-built Mrs. Ayres opened one diamond and the vicar's wife went straight to four spades. This was too high for Brother Lucius, who led the ace of clubs when no further bidding resulted. East followed with the queen, clearly a singleton, and Brother Lucius's first thought was to continue with king and another club. If his partner held, say, the ten of trumps, he could blast a hole in declarer's trump holding.

Since the hand might decide the match, Brother Lucius paused to consider another line of defence. What if he switched immediately to his singleton diamond? Yes. Then he could win the first round of trumps, underlead his club to put partner on lead, and ruff the diamond return. This defence seemed more promising, requiring only that East should hold two trumps.

When Brother Lucius switched to a diamond, the risk of a ruff was all too obvious to Mrs. Pritchett. Provided West held the ace of trumps, though, it might be possible to thwart the defenders by playing ace and another heart immediately. If East failed to put in an honour, declarer could throw her club loser and break the link between the defenders' hands.

"Ace of hearts, please, Phyllis," said Mrs. Pritchett, not too pleased to see Brother Lucius contribute the king to this trick. "And a small heart, please."

Brother Paulo, well aware of declarer's intentions, covered dummy's seven with the jack and the contract was doomed. Mrs. Pritchett discarded her club, hoping West held king–queen alone in hearts. It was not to be. East's jack held the trick and the ensuing diamond ruff put the game one down.

"Any good?" said the Abbot as his other pair returned. "We picked up about fifteen in this room, I make it."

"They played quite well against us, actually," replied Brother Lucius. "We did beat four spades on board 31, though. Is that any use?"

The monastery team had won the match by 7 IMPs, much to the delight of the last minute stand-in, Brother Sextus.

"Two more green points!" he exclaimed. "Do you know, Abbot, I believe that makes me a six-star regional master."

"Yes, you played a sound game," replied the Abbot. "Unfortunately, of course, the greens will have to go to Brother Xavier. You were ineligible for the match and if the E.B.U. ever found out, I hate to think what . . ."

The Abbot's voice disintegrated into a contrived cough as the vicar's wife entered the room.

"We make it 7 points to you," said Mrs. Pritchett. "A little disappointing, I must say, in view of the results at our table. Mona Godfrey had one of her *mal de têtes*, apparently." She paused to sign the match result card. "Is there anything I can offer you before you leave?"

"I couldn't eat a thing after that excellent tea," replied the Abbot. "Unless . . . did I hear you say there were still some fish-paste sandwiches left?"

26

The Abbot Restores the Balance

Although the Abbot liked to encourage postulants who showed some aptitude for the game, matters had drifted out of hand recently. Not only had Brother Damien and Brother Mark qualified for the final of the National Pairs, they had also had the impudence to win the Thursday night pairs game two weeks running.

"Ah, Brother Lucius," said the Abbot one sunny morning on the chapel steps. "Can you partner me next Thursday in the pairs? After the last two results, I'm most anxious to restore the authority of the senior players."

"That would indeed be a pleasure, Abbot," replied Brother Lucius. "Unfortunately I've already agreed to play with Brother Xavier. Some other time, perhaps?"

"Brother Xavier will be unavailable. I've just assigned him to the evening duty guarding the soft-fruit allotment," declared the Abbot. "I'll put us down on the entry sheet."

The following Thursday, the Abbot and Brother Lucius had made a successful start to the evening when the young pair were spotted approaching the table. "Right, Lucius. Battle stations," announced the Abbot.

The two postulants sat down nervously, placing their neatly-scribed convention cards on the table.

"These two lads have been showing some promise, I'm told," remarked the Abbot to his partner. "It shows my lectures to the novitiate don't pass entirely unnoticed."

The first hand saw the Abbot in 3 NT:

E–W game, dealer North

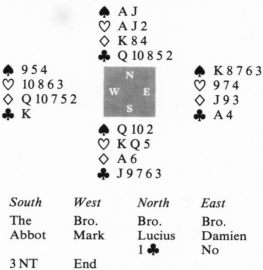

♠ A J
♡ A J 2
◇ K 8 4
♣ Q 10 8 5 2

♠ 9 5 4
♡ 10 8 6 3
◇ Q 10 7 5 2
♣ K

♠ K 8 7 6 3
♡ 9 7 4
◇ J 9 3
♣ A 4

♠ Q 10 2
♡ K Q 5
◇ A 6
♣ J 9 7 6 3

South	West	North	East
The	Bro.	Bro.	Bro.
Abbot	Mark	Lucius	Damien
		1 ♣	No
3 NT	End		

Brother Mark led the two of diamonds and the Abbot observed that there were two club honours to knock out and only two stops in the diamond suit.

"Fourth best leads, presumably," he said, raising his eyebrows in Brother Damien's direction.

"No, we're playing third and fifth, Abbot," came the studious reply. "There was an article in a French magazine recently which . . ."

The Abbot cut him short with a disapproving wave of the hand. "In future you will confine yourselves to fourth best, like the rest of the monastery," he informed them. "And kindly don't embark on any further unorthodoxies without my permission."

"Shall I take the card back and replace it with my fourth best?" asked Brother Mark, with such an innocent expression that the Abbot couldn't tell if he was being insolent.

Deciding to give him the benefit of the doubt, the Abbot turned his attention to the 3 NT contract and soon spotted a promising line. He must duck the first round of diamonds, win the second and then force out the first club honour. The defenders could now clear the diamond suit, but if the player who won the second club trick had no diamonds left, the contract would be secure. Anxious to give his young opponents a lesson in accurate dummy play, the Abbot played low from dummy and allowed East's jack to hold the trick.

[136]

Brother Damien adjusted his spectacles thoughtfully. Declarer's diamond holding was obviously A x rather than Q x, or he would surely have captured the first trick. And if he was ducking from A x, he presumably had two losers in the club suit. Well, in that case there should be time to get the spades moving. Brother Damien abandoned the diamond suit and switched to a small spade.

The Abbot looked distastefully at this unexpected card and won the trick with dummy's jack. A club to West's king was followed in quick time by the removal of dummy's ace of spades, and Brother Damien cashed three spade tricks when he came in with the club ace.

"No need to duck the first round of diamonds rather than the second, is there, Abbot?" queried Brother Lucius. "That could gain only if diamonds were 6–2, a distribution precluded by the opening lead."

"No doubt you understand these new-fangled conventions better than I do," replied the Abbot sourly. "Shall we proceed?"

On the next hand the Abbot picked up a miserable 1-count but nevertheless ended as declarer.

Love all, dealer West

♠ A K 7 5
♡ 6
♢ A K 10 8 2
♣ K 8 5

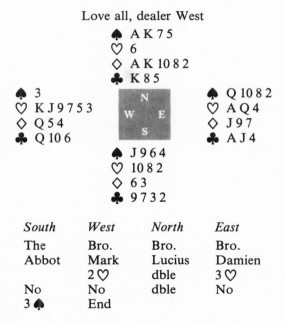

♠ 3
♡ K J 9 7 5 3
♢ Q 5 4
♣ Q 10 6

♠ Q 10 8 2
♡ A Q 4
♢ J 9 7
♣ A J 4

♠ J 9 6 4
♡ 10 8 2
♢ 6 3
♣ 9 7 3 2

South	West	North	East
The	Bro.	Bro.	Bro.
Abbot	Mark	Lucius	Damien
	2 ♡	dble	3 ♡
No	No	dble	No
3 ♠	End		

Brother Mark led the seven of hearts to his partner's ace and Brother Damien continued the suit, forcing the dummy to ruff. The

Abbot cashed the ace of spades and the top diamond honours and ruffed a diamond to hand, setting up the suit. He next ruffed his last heart and cashed the king of spades, observing the 4–1 break with a philosophical shake of the head. Hoping that something would develop, he led the ten of diamonds to this end position:

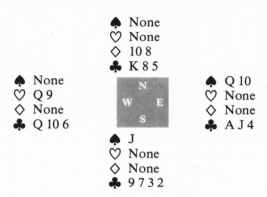

                    ♠ None
                    ♡ None
                    ♢ 10 8
                    ♣ K 8 5

    ♠ None   ♠ Q 10
    ♡ Q 9   N   ♡ None
    ♢ None   W   E   ♢ None
    ♣ Q 10 6   S   ♣ A J 4

                    ♠ J
                    ♡ None
                    ♢ None
                    ♣ 9 7 3 2

Brother Damien ruffed with the ten, and the Abbot saw there was little to be gained by overruffing. Even if the ace of clubs was onside, the defenders would still be able to take the remaining four tricks. He therefore discarded a club instead. Brother Damien played the queen of spades to pull declarer's last trump but then had to give the dummy two tricks, the king of clubs and the last diamond. + 140 proved to be an excellent score for the Abbot's side.

"Better to ruff high, isn't it?" suggested Brother Mark to his partner. "Then you can exit with the ten of spades to declarer's jack and we take the last three club tricks."

"Yes, that defence would doubtless be good enough against most declarers," conceded the Abbot. "On this occasion, though, I would underruff with the jack to avoid being endplayed. You can make the ten of trumps now, but you still have to give dummy two tricks at the end."

The two postulants nodded their admiration of this line of play.

"Is that right, Abbot?" queried Brother Lucius. "If you underruff, can't East simply exit with a club, keeping his trump to deal with dummy's last diamond?"

"I think the analysis is getting a bit deep for these two youngsters," said the Abbot, indicating with his finger that it was time for Lucius to fill in the travelling score slip. "Anyhow, I imagine East–West will be making 3 NT at most tables."

[138]

27

Brother Xavier's Bonfire

"That's a splendid bonfire you've got going there, Brother Xavier," cried the Abbot, gazing down from the card-room window at the billowing smoke. "I hope you remembered my instructions to check whether Mrs. Mears-Glossop had any washing out before you lit it."

"Yes, Abbot," shouted Brother Xavier, tossing another armful of leaves into the blaze. "She had a full two lines of sheets and other things out, and the wind is blowing in just the right direction to catch them."

"Good!" exclaimed the Abbot, as he closed the leaded window. "That'll teach her to complain to the Council about the chapel bells sounding at the 4 a.m. prayer."

Resuming his seat at the £1 table, the Abbot found the next hand already dealt.

East–West game, dealer West

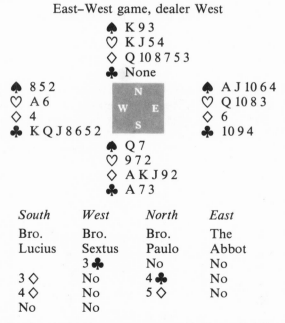

```
              ♠ K 9 3
              ♡ K J 5 4
              ◇ Q 10 8 7 5 3
              ♣ None
♠ 8 5 2                        ♠ A J 10 6 4
♡ A 6            N             ♡ Q 10 8 3
◇ 4          W     E           ◇ 6
♣ K Q J 8 6 5 2    S           ♣ 10 9 4
              ♠ Q 7
              ♡ 9 7 2
              ◇ A K J 9 2
              ♣ A 7 3
```

South	West	North	East
Bro.	Bro.	Bro.	The
Lucius	Sextus	Paulo	Abbot
	3 ♣	No	No
3 ◇	No	4 ♣	No
4 ◇	No	5 ◇	No
No	No		

Brother Lucius decided to protect on a minimum holding and was soon whisked by his partner into a dubious diamond game. Still,

[139]

thought Brother Lucius as he ruffed the opening club lead in dummy, they would have made three clubs so five diamonds is quite a good sacrifice in a way.

West could hardly hold both heart honours on the bidding, so the only genuine chance of making the contract seemed to be to find him with the queen–ten doubleton, or with a singleton queen or ace, when an endplay on East might be possible. Brother Lucius picked up the two outstanding trumps with his ace and led a small heart from hand. Only a disappointing six-spot showed on his left, so he boldly went up with the king and returned a small spade. The Abbot played the 10 and South won with the queen.

Brother Lucius now ruffed his remaining small club and returned to hand with a trump. A spade was discarded on the ace of clubs and he exited with a spade to the Abbot's ace. The defenders were hopelessly entangled and two tricks later Brother Sextus had to give a ruff-and-discard.

"What a moronic defence!" cried the Abbot. "Surely it's obvious to go in with the ace of hearts and play another heart?"

"Well, it's obvious enough now, Abbot," replied Brother Sextus. "But I certainly didn't find it so at the time. Why shouldn't declarer hold ♠ Q J x and two small hearts?"

"Most unlikely," declared the Abbot. "Why is it that every time you make a ludicrous mistake you try to conjure up some wild distribution to justify it?"

Brother Sextus lapsed into silence. The Abbot was quite impregnable in the post-mortem, everyone knew that. The more reasonable one's arguments, the more dismissively he would wave them aside.

The rubbers ticked by without anyone winning very much, and then the Abbot dealt himself this solid-looking spade game:

Game all, dealer South

```
              ♠ 8 6 5
              ♡ Q J 6
              ◇ 9 7 5 3
              ♣ Q J 3
  ♠ J 3                        ♠ 9 7 4
  ♡ K 10 9 5 4 2    N          ♡ 8 7 3
  ◇ Q          W       E       ◇ A J 10 2
  ♣ 7 6 5 2         S          ♣ 10 8 4
              ♠ A K Q 10 2
              ♡ A
              ◇ K 8 6 4
              ♣ A K 9
```

South	West	North	East
The	Bro.	Bro.	Bro.
Abbot	Lucius	Sextus	Paulo
2 ♣	No	2 ◇	No
2 ♠	No	2 NT	No
3 ◇	No	3 ♠	No
4 ♠	No	No	No

Brother Lucius made the rather wild lead of the singleton queen of diamonds, won by his partner's ace. Brother Paulo returned a cunning two of diamonds and the Abbot stepped in unawares with his king, ruffed by West.

The Abbot captured West's trump exit in hand and drew two more rounds. There remained one plausible chance of bringing home the contract. If West held the king of hearts and no more than three clubs, he could be subjected to a throw-in after his clubs had been extracted. The Abbot marked time by cashing his last two trumps but Brother Lucius continued to throw hearts, holding on steadfastly to every one of his precious clubs.

After taking the ace of hearts and the three top club honours, the Abbot threw Brother Lucius in with a heart, but the cleverly preserved two of clubs spelt doom to the contract.

"Oh, bad luck, Abbot," said Brother Sextus dubiously, "but er . . . why did you put up the king of diamonds at trick two?"

"What a stupid question," grunted the Abbot. "If I duck the return and West has led from the Q J 10 of diamonds, he can give his partner a ruff. And for all I know I might still have to lose another trump trick."

"Only if East is ruffing with a singleton trump," persisted Brother Sextus. "That would be rather a wild distribution, surely?"

"Well, it all paved the way for the truly remarkable throw-in that followed," declared the Abbot. "Most unlucky to find Lucius with the long club, I must say."

"Why don't you write it up for the monastery newsletter, Abbot?" said Brother Sextus, tongue in cheek. "Give East the nine of diamonds so you have to play the king at trick two, and give him the long club too, so that your throw-in proves successful."

"Yes, I need a hand for next week's article actually," replied the Abbot, whose bridge column contained little else but his own brilliancies.

"And you could round off the article by mentioning another line of play," suggested Brother Lucius. "Take just two rounds of clubs, the ace and queen, and then exit with the heart queen, throwing the king of clubs from hand. That line makes even if West does hold the long club."

The Abbot paused for thought, then delivered a black glance in Brother Lucius's direction. "A double-dummy line," he declared. "In any case, we should have been in 3 NT. Didn't you see that you had a sure guard in each of the unbid suits, partner?"

Suddenly there was a jangling sound from the ancient wall-telephone.

"It's for you, Abbot," called Brother Aelred, who was waiting to cut in at one of the 5p tables.

"Can't you see I'm busy?" replied the Abbot, cutting the cards ready for the next deal. "Who is it, anyway?"

"It's someone from the Council apparently," said Brother Aelred. "Says he wants to speak to you about a bonfire."

28

Brother Aelred's Winning Line

Brother Zac entered the Abbot's study and observed his superior hard at work behind a desk covered in papers.

"Er . . . sorry to interrupt you, Abbot, but will a 9-table Howell be all right for tomorrow's Simultaneous Pairs?"

Without looking up, the Abbot held aloft a sheet of paper covered in copperplate handwriting.

"Ah, thank you, Abbot," said Brother Zac, studying the sheet carefully. "I see. A Mitchell movement."

"Yes, I've put all the strong pairs East–West this year, just for a change," replied the Abbot. "I've also brought in some postulants from my beginners' class to weaken the North–South line."

"They matchpoint this one over the whole country, don't they?" said Brother Zac, smiling at the Abbot's cleverness. "Oh dear! I see you've put me in the North–South line."

"Did I?" replied the Abbot, returning to his previous paperwork. "Well, I didn't want to make the scheme too obvious."

The following evening the cardroom was alive with the special atmosphere that accompanies a Charity Pairs. Several kibitzers were in attendance at the Abbot's table.

N–S game, dealer South

```
              ♠ 7 6 4
              ♡ 9 6 2
              ◇ J
              ♣ Q J 9 7 6 4
♠ A J 5 2        ┌─────────┐      ♠ 8
♡ A 4            │    N    │      ♡ Q J 8 5
◇ A 8 3          │  W   E  │      ◇ 10 9 7 5 4
♣ K 10 3 2       │    S    │      ♣ A 8 5
                 └─────────┘
              ♠ K Q 10 9 3
              ♡ K 10 7 3
              ◇ K Q 6 2
              ♣ None
```

South	West	North	East
Bro.	The	Bro.	Bro.
Adam	Abbot	Cameron	Paulo
1 ♠	1 NT	No	No
2 ♡	No	No	Dble
No	No	2 ♠	No
No	Dble	End	

Well satisfied with the auction's path, the Abbot led a low trump against two spades doubled. The 17-year-old Brother Adam, who had entered the novitiate only three months previously, won in hand and led a low diamond.

The Abbot stepped in with the ace and continued with ace and another trump, sacrificing a trump trick which he hoped would return with interest later in the play. Declarer drew a fourth round of trumps, then led a heart to the 9 and jack. The ace of clubs was ruffed by declarer, and a low heart went to West's bare ace. The Abbot, sitting West, was now on lead in this end position:

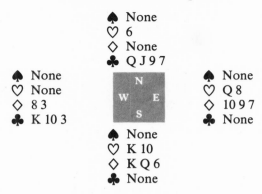

His lead of the king of clubs squeezed East in the red suits, and Brother Adam made the last four tricks for his contract.

"Surely that should go down," declared the Abbot. "What if I exit with a diamond at the end, instead of cashing the club king?"

"No better, I think," replied Brother Paulo. "Declarer is putting me in with the fourth round of diamonds to give him two hearts."

"There must be some way to beat it," continued the Abbot. "What if I duck the diamond at trick 2? Is that any use?"

"H'm. Dummy's jack is winning, club ruff to hand, king of diamonds covered and ruffed, one more club ruff to hand . . ."

Brother Paulo reached for his scorecard and scribbled this end position on the back:

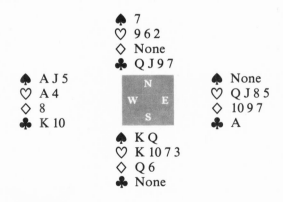

"Now if declarer plays queen and another diamond, he will make only one more trick. West will ruff with the jack, cash the ace of trumps and exit in a black suit, putting the contract one down."

Brother Paulo continued to study the end position. "Ah, I see it!" he said. "Declarer must take his diamond ruff first, ruff another club to hand and then exit with the queen of diamonds. Yes, West makes three trump tricks but has to give declarer the king of hearts at the end."

Brother Cameron entered the 670 on the scoresheet with an apologetic air. "It was very kind of you to arrange this movement, Abbot," he said.

"What do you mean?" grunted the Abbot.

"Well, you know, to let us postulants play against all the best pairs."

"Yes," agreed Brother Adam. "It's a very valuable experience hearing you analyse the hands like this."

"I dare say," replied the Abbot, "but it has nothing to do with me. Brother Zac is in charge of the movement."

With one round to go, the Abbot estimated his score at 54% locally, which would surely stretch to well over 60% nationally. He was further encouraged by the sight of Brother Aelred and his partner waiting for them on the last table.

"Having a good session, Brother Aelred?" enquired the Abbot, as he took his seat.

"Not too bad, thank you, Abbot," replied Brother Aelred. "We've had quite a few plus scores. Two very poor ones against Brother Lucius, unfortunately."

The Abbot winced at this piece of information. The first hand was disappointingly flat in 3 NT. The second saw Brother Aelred in four hearts.

Brother Aelred's Winning Line

Love all, dealer West

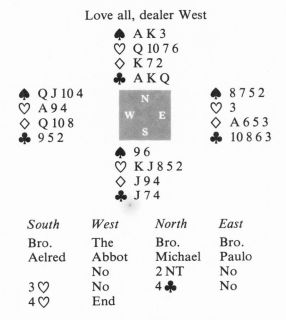

North
- ♠ A K 3
- ♡ Q 10 7 6
- ◇ K 7 2
- ♣ A K Q

West
- ♠ Q J 10 4
- ♡ A 9 4
- ◇ Q 10 8
- ♣ 9 5 2

East
- ♠ 8 7 5 2
- ♡ 3
- ◇ A 6 5 3
- ♣ 10 8 6 3

South
- ♠ 9 6
- ♡ K J 8 5 2
- ◇ J 9 4
- ♣ J 7 4

South	West	North	East
Bro.	The	Bro.	Bro.
Aelred	Abbot	Michael	Paulo
	No	2 NT	No
3 ♡	No	4 ♣	No
4 ♡	End		

"What was this four-club bid?" said Brother Aelred, inspecting the dummy with a puzzled air.

"I thought we agreed to play Gerber after a no-trump opening," replied his partner. "If you'd shown two aces, I was going to bid the slam."

Brother Aelred took the spade lead in dummy and forced out the ace of trumps. He won the spade continuation, drew trumps and ruffed dummy's last spade in hand. He was about to lead a diamond towards dummy, when it occurred to him that it might be beneficial to cash the clubs before playing on diamonds. Three rounds of clubs left him in dummy. He now played a low diamond to the nine and ten.

The Abbot exited with the eight of diamonds and Brother Aelred had a crucial guess to make. A memory stirred from an old magazine that Brother Lucius had lent him a while back.

"Yes, of course," he murmured. "I remember. Low, please."

"Oh, well guessed, partner!" exclaimed Brother Michael when East's ace appeared and Brother Aelred claimed the contract. "Another plus score!"

"I'm afraid you gave the game away there, Brother Paulo," said Brother Aelred. "You discarded your fourth diamond earlier on, didn't you?"

"How careless of me," replied Brother Paulo in a good-humoured tone. "May I enquire what difference that made to your play?"

"Reese's Bols bridge tip!" replied Brother Aelred. "I can't remember why, but he said a defender was much more likely to discard from A x x x than from Q x x x."

The Abbot opened the scoresheet and was puzzled to find that only one other pair had made the contract.

Brother Paulo was less surprised. "The best play in diamonds is low to dummy's 7," he said, "hoping to duck the trick to East. That is succeeding immediately if East has the 8 or West has the ace. And even if you are unlucky and the first round goes 4–8–king–ace, you can still guess right on the return."

"Yes, that must be best," agreed the Abbot. "It fails as the cards lie, of course."

"Do you mean I found the only winning line, Abbot?" asked a delighted Brother Aelred.

"Yes indeed," replied the Abbot, rising to his feet. "It's essential to forget to cash the clubs until the last minute. It's equally important to completely misapply Reese's Bols bridge tip. Not surprisingly, only one other declarer seems to have managed it."

29

The Testing of Brother James

Brother Damien, the most promising card player among the postulants, knocked timidly on the oak door of the Abbot's study.

"Enter!" came a heavy voice from within.

"I'm so sorry to interrupt you, Abbot."

"Yes?" said the Abbot, looking up from a desk strewn with paperwork. "What is it?"

"Well, we've had rather a good idea in the novitiate, Abbot, and I was volunteered to put it to you."

"You were volunteered?" winced the Abbot. "You were *elected* to put it to me, you mean. Well?"

"We thought we could hold a special pairs event where each postulant was partnered by one of the more senior monks."

"H'm. Not a bad idea," replied the Abbot, consulting a leather-bound desk diary. "There's nothing on next Friday, it seems."

"Doesn't Brother Michael hold his bible-reading classes on Friday evenings?"

The Abbot hesitated for a moment. "I have detected signs of staleness there," he said. "I will speak to Brother Michael. Now, let's set the ball rolling. Shall I put the two of us down as the first pair?"

"That would indeed be an honour, Abbot," replied Brother Damien. "But wouldn't it be fairer if there were a draw for partners? Fairer to the other postulants, I mean."

"As you wish," said the Abbot, closing the discussion with a wave of the hand.

The following Friday the Abbot stood at one end of the novices' cardroom drawing names in turn from two silver vases traditionally used for the purpose.

"Pair number 5," he announced. "Brother Lucius and . . ." those postulants who had not yet been drawn held their breath, praying that they might be lucky, ". . . and Brother Mark."

Brother Mark beamed modestly as his colleagues congratulated him. A few more pairs were drawn but the Abbot's name had not yet appeared and those postulants remaining in the draw were looking increasingly apprehensive.

"Pair number 11 . . . ah!" the Abbot removed his glasses and looked up. "My good self, at last. Now, let's see who's the lucky . . . or should I say the unlucky one?" The Abbot paused so that the gathering could savour his jest. "Ah, it's Brother James."

Brother James, one of the less able members of the Abbot's beginners' class, gave a brave smile. The draw was soon completed, and Brother James could feel his heart beating as the first hand was dealt.

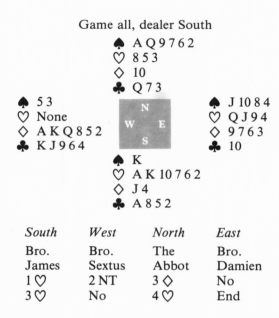

Game all, dealer South

            ♠ A Q 9 7 6 2
            ♡ 8 5 3
            ◇ 10
            ♣ Q 7 3
♠ 5 3   ♠ J 10 8 4
♡ None   ♡ Q J 9 4
◇ A K Q 8 5 2   ◇ 9 7 6 3
♣ K J 9 6 4   ♣ 10
            ♠ K
            ♡ A K 10 7 6 2
            ◇ J 4
            ♣ A 8 5 2

South	West	North	East
Bro.	Bro.	The	Bro.
James	Sextus	Abbot	Damien
1 ♡	2 NT	3 ◇	No
3 ♡	No	4 ♡	End

"I was trying you out, there," said the Abbot jovially. "As Brother Sextus had shown both the minors, my three diamond bid was conventional, indicating a good suit of spades and moderate support for hearts."

"Er, yes, quite so," murmured Brother James, stroking the bristles of an incipient beard as he inspected the dummy. "A brilliant call, Abbot."

The Abbot nodded amiably and waved a finger at the dummy, indicating that Brother James should proceed with the play. When the ace of diamonds held the trick, West switched to a spade, won in hand by declarer. The ace of hearts revealed the bad trump break, and Brother James crossed to dummy with a diamond ruff.

There was no point in leading a trump now, because East would split his honours and there was no further entry to dummy. Instead,

Brother James turned to the spade suit. If they were 3–3 he could throw all his club losers and East would have to ruff the fourth round with a trump trick.

It was not to be. West discarded on the third round of spades and declarer eventually lost two trumps, a diamond and a club.

"It was a difficult hand," said the Abbot, with what he believed was a friendly smile. "But surely the only danger to the contract was a 4–0 trump break. You should have won the second trick with dummy's ace of spades and led a heart to the ten."

"No, I couldn't do that, Abbot. I had two club losers," replied Brother James. "I needed the ace–queen of spades for two club discards."

"You need only one discard on the spades," explained the Abbot. "Win the second trick with the ace of spades and lead a trump. If East splits his honours, you win, ruff a diamond, discard a club on the queen of spades and lead another trump. You lose a heart, a diamond and a club."

A round or two later Brother Lucius and Brother Mark arrived at the table. The Abbot's welcoming smile belied a steely determination to outgun his rival. Brother James played the first hand in 1 NT for an average score. This was the second hand:

E–W game, dealer South

	♠ 10 5 3	
	♡ K 10 7	
	◇ K Q J 5	
	♣ K 6 3	

♠ K Q 9		♠ 4
♡ J 8 3	N	♡ 9 6 5 2
◇ 9 7 6 2	W E	◇ 10 8 4 3
♣ 10 9 7	S	♣ Q J 4 2

	♠ A J 8 7 6 2	
	♡ A Q 4	
	◇ A	
	♣ A 8 5	

South	West	North	East
The	Bro.	Bro.	Bro.
Abbot	Mark	James	Lucius
2 ♣	No	2 NT	No
3 ♠	No	4 NT	No
5 NT	No	6 ♠	

When the six spade call ran to Brother Mark in the West seat, he studied his hand uncertainly. "Was the 4 NT bid Blackwood, Abbot?" he enquired.

"Unless we agreed to play the Culbertson 4–5," replied the Abbot, making heavy-handed play of studying his convention card. "No, I see here that we are playing Blackwood."

Brother Mark eyed his trump holding once more. So, the spade ace was definitely on his right. He recalled an S. J. Simon story about a lady who hadn't doubled him in 7 NT despite being on lead with an ace in hand. She had then underled the ace and allowed the contract to make. They were bound to laugh at him if he made the same sort of mistake. "My bid, is it?" he said hesitantly. "Er . . . double."

There was no further bidding and the Abbot won the ten of clubs lead in hand. The double was presumably based on trump tricks, and since he could not deal with a 4–0 break, the Abbot decided to aim at a trump reduction that might catch K Q x. He cashed the ace of diamonds and finessed the ten of hearts, hoping to gain an extra entry to dummy. When this manoeuvre succeeded, the Abbot smiled to himself. If Lucius had held the West cards, he would doubtless have inserted the jack to kill the extra entry. After discarding a club on the king of diamonds, the Abbot ruffed the queen of diamonds in hand. He then cashed the ace of clubs and used dummy's remaining kings to gain entry for two further minor-suit ruffs.

When all this passed off successfully, the Abbot gazed triumphantly at his three remaining cards – ♠ A J 8. When the 8 of spades was led, West played low in the vain hope that his partner might hold the singleton jack. The Abbot's momentary panic was soon quelled when dummy's ten held the trick.

"Just the twelve, partner," said the Abbot, reaching casually for his scorecard. "What do you make that, Lucius? 1210, is it?"

Brother Mark scratched his head. "I wasn't wrong to double, was I?" he asked.

"With two trump tricks *and* the jack of hearts?" replied the Abbot, with a prodigious wink in the direction of Brother Lucius. "Of course not!"

30

Inspector Bulstrode Recovers

The Hampshire police team had recently been promoted to the first division of the County League. Their opening fixture was a home match against the monastery team.

"Evenin' all," said the Abbot, giving the duty sergeant a mock salute.

The sergeant smiled wearily. "You must be the gentlemen for the bridge match," he said. "The Inspector said you should go straight down. You're playing in the last two cells on the left."

Inspector Bulstrode, a large man with a ginger moustache, greeted the monks with an apology about the playing conditions. "We normally play our matches upstairs in the canteen," he said, "but they're using it to check out some films that were confiscated today down in St. Mary's Road."

"Why can't they do that in one of the cells and let us play upstairs?" said P.C. Godhill.

"Be sensible, lad," replied the Inspector. "You couldn't fit forty blokes in one of these cells."

The match was soon under way.

N–S game, dealer North

♠ Q 8 7 5 2
♡ K Q 9 5
♢ A 9
♣ A 10

♠ 10 3		♠ A J 9
♡ 6 4	**N**	♡ J 10 7 2
♢ K Q J 10 8 7 4 2	**W** **E**	♢ 6 3
♣ 5	**S**	♣ 8 4 3 2

♠ K 6 4
♡ A 8 3
♢ 5
♣ K Q J 9 7 6

South	*West*	*North*	*East*
Inspector	The	P.C.	Bro.
Bulstrode	Abbot	Godhill	Lucius
		1 ♠	No
2 ♣	3 ♢	3 ♡	No
3 ♠	No	4 ♣	No
4 NT	No	5 ♡	No
6 ♣	No	No	No

The Abbot, who had expected better hospitality than an unpleasant-smelling cell, led the king of diamonds against six clubs. The Inspector won in dummy, drew trumps in four rounds and led a spade to the queen. Brother Lucius, sitting East, could see an easy squeeze for declarer if he took the trick. He therefore allowed the queen to win, following smoothly with the nine.

The Inspector tested the heart suit unsuccessfully and then ducked a spade, reckoning that his only chance was to find West with the bare ace. Brother Lucius won with the jack and cashed the ace to put declarer one down.

The Inspector blinked at Brother Lucius in disbelief. "How can *you* have the ace of spades?" he demanded.

"There's no law against it, is there?" said Brother Lucius, feigning concern. "Your partner would be an accomplice, even so. He dealt the cards."

Young P.C. Godhill, a keen analyst, caught his partner's attention. "Interesting situation that, George. I wonder how it would be if after the spade to the queen you led a spade back to the king? Nothing's lost if West does win with a doubleton ace, because then you can squeeze East in the majors."

The Inspector lit a cigarette and slipped it under his ginger moustache. "Don't call me George here in the station," he said, pausing to puff out a large cloud of smoke. "It's against regulations."

"Sorry, Inspector."

"I don't mind it on away matches, lad, but regulations are regulations."

This was the last board of the first half:

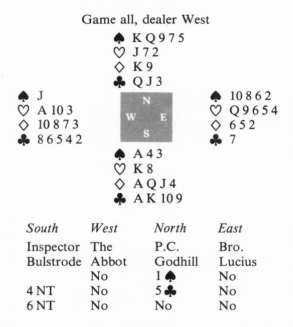

Game all, dealer West

North
♠ K Q 9 7 5
♡ J 7 2
◇ K 9
♣ Q J 3

West
♠ J
♡ A 10 3
◇ 10 8 7 3
♣ 8 6 5 4 2

East
♠ 10 8 6 2
♡ Q 9 6 5 4
◇ 6 5 2
♣ 7

South
♠ A 4 3
♡ K 8
◇ A Q J 4
♣ A K 10 9

South	West	North	East
Inspector	The	P.C.	Bro.
Bulstrode	Abbot	Godhill	Lucius
	No	1 ♠	No
4 NT	No	5 ♣	No
6 NT	No	No	No

Once again the Inspector decided against a slam in his partner's suit, this time to protect his king of hearts. The Abbot led the jack of spades against six no-trumps and declarer won on the table. He now played a second round of spades to the ace and the Abbot discarded a club, a move he was later to regret. The Inspector cashed eight minor-suit tricks in quick succession to leave this ending:

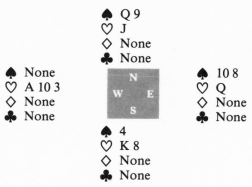

```
              ♠ Q 9
              ♡ J
              ◇ None
              ♣ None
♠ None                        ♠ 10 8
♡ A 10 3        N             ♡ Q
◇ None        W   E           ◇ None
♣ None          S             ♣ None
              ♠ 4
              ♡ K 8
              ◇ None
              ♣ None
```

When he exited with the 8 of hearts, the contract was assured whichever heart honour East held.

"That should make up for the other one, partner," said the Inspector, well pleased with himself.

"We might have beaten that," said the Abbot grumpily. "It looks silly but if I keep all my clubs we have a chance."

Brother Lucius nodded his agreement. "It's not often that five clubs to the eight are worth keeping," he said. "The board will be flat, I expect. Unless they play it in spades, of course."

"Can we get you a drink?" asked the Inspector.

The Abbot looked up with interest. "Yes, indeed," he replied. "Perhaps you've a consignment of bottles from Southampton docks that requires testing?"

"That'll be the day," said the constable, rising to his feet. "Does everyone take milk and sugar?"

At half-time the Abbot was disturbed to find that the scores were level. "Must you smoke?" he grunted, as the two detectives resumed their seats. "These cells seem to have no ventilation at all."

"They are a bit lacking in the basic comforts," agreed Detective Sergeant Burke, sending a column of smoke rings towards the ceiling. "Odd you should mind that, though, being monks."

Love all, dealer North

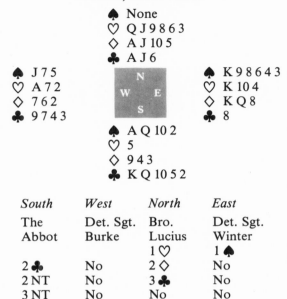

♠ None
♡ Q J 9 8 6 3
◊ A J 10 5
♣ A J 6

♠ J 7 5
♡ A 7 2
◊ 7 6 2
♣ 9 7 4 3

♠ K 9 8 6 4 3
♡ K 10 4
◊ K Q 8
♣ 8

♠ A Q 10 2
♡ 5
◊ 9 4 3
♣ K Q 10 5 2

South	West	North	East
The	Det. Sgt.	Bro.	Det. Sgt.
Abbot	Burke	Lucius	Winter
		1 ♡	1 ♠
2 ♣	No	2 ◊	No
2 NT	No	3 ♣	No
3 NT	No	No	No

Detective Sergeant Burke led the five of spades to the king and ace. The Abbot could count eight top tricks with good prospects of a quick ninth trick in diamonds. A finesse of dummy's jack of diamonds lost to the queen and East returned the six of spades.

Placing West with J x x rather than three low cards, the Abbot played the two from hand. After winning with the seven, Burke stubbed out his cigarette butt and paused for thought. Declarer was obviously missing the king of hearts or he would have led the suit by now. He also seemed to have started with ♠ A Q 10 x or ♠ A Q 9 x. With the latter holding, though, he would probably have played for a block in the spade suit by rising with the queen on the second round. Burke placed another cigarette in his mouth and reached for his Swan Vestas. There was only one defence to trouble declarer, he concluded. A diamond!

The Abbot was not pleased to see the six of diamonds appear. He now had to make a decision in diamonds before leading the queen of spades to see if the jack would fall. Unwilling to be tricked out of his original 75% chance, the Abbot took a second diamond finesse and went one down when the defenders cashed two heart tricks.

[157]

"How were the spades?" demanded the Abbot.

"I had jack to three, actually," replied Detective Sergeant Burke, puffing triumphantly at his cigarette. "I was afraid that would be all too obvious when I put the second diamond through."

The Abbot glared at him through the smoke. "I played according to the odds," he said.

Brother Lucius made no comment, though it occurred to him that the Abbot could have improved his chances by ducking the *first* round of spades. He could then win the next round, finesse in diamonds, win the next spade with the ace and have a second diamond finesse in reserve.

The penultimate set of boards ended without further incident and the two detectives left the room. The Abbot was just enjoying his third cup of tea when in swept the Chairwoman of the Prison Visitors Association, Mrs. Gloria de Lionville.

"Good gracious!" she exclaimed. "What are you doing in here?"

"You may well ask," replied the Abbot with feeling. "According to Inspector Bulstrode the crime squad carried out a raid this morning and picked up some films of a dubious nature . . ."

"A patently absurd trumped-up charge!" declared Mrs. de Lionville. "Who ever heard of monks being involved in a blue film racket? Now, tell me, have you contacted a solicitor?"

Light dawned on the Abbot. "We are beyond help, madam, I assure you," he said, gazing sadly out of the cell window. "Having erred, we must accept our due punishment with fortitude."

"You'll need a solicitor," insisted Mrs. de Lionville. "I'll contact my own man at once. Wait here."

"We have no alternative, madam," replied the Abbot.

When Brother Paulo and Brother Xavier returned, a hasty comparison revealed that the monastery team was now 14 IMPs in arrears.

"Just play a steady game, for heaven's sake," said the Abbot as his other pair prepared to leave. "Lucius and I will pick up the points we need."

Inspector Bulstrode and P.C. Godhill returned and battle recommenced.

Inspector Bulstrode Recovers

N–S game, dealer West

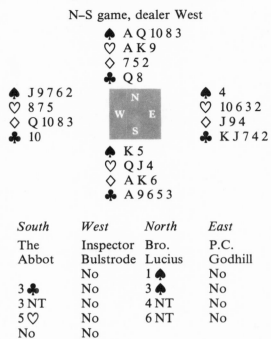

North
- ♠ A Q 10 8 3
- ♡ A K 9
- ♢ 7 5 2
- ♣ Q 8

West
- ♠ J 9 7 6 2
- ♡ 8 7 5
- ♢ Q 10 8 3
- ♣ 10

East
- ♠ 4
- ♡ 10 6 3 2
- ♢ J 9 4
- ♣ K J 7 4 2

South
- ♠ K 5
- ♡ Q J 4
- ♢ A K 6
- ♣ A 9 6 5 3

South	West	North	East
The Abbot	Inspector Bulstrode	Bro. Lucius	P.C. Godhill
	No	1 ♠	No
3 ♣	No	3 ♠	No
3 NT	No	4 NT	No
5 ♡	No	6 NT	No
No	No		

The slam was somewhat less than cold, observed the Abbot as the dummy went down. He won the heart lead in hand and led a club to the ten, queen and king. P.C. Godhill immediately returned a club, hoping to put the Abbot to a decision in this suit before the bad spade break came to light. On the present hand it made no difference because declarer needed a second club trick even if the spades were all good.

Applying the Principle of Restricted Choice (from J 10 West might have played the jack), the Abbot ran the club return successfully to dummy's 8. Since West's club shortage suggested length in spades, he next crossed to the king of spades and boldly finessed the ten of spades. East showed out, glancing hopefully at the Abbot to see if he looked annoyed.

"In that case, the rest are mine," declared the Abbot, facing his cards with a flourish. Inspector Bulstrode surveyed the evidence suspiciously. "Four spades, three hearts, two diamonds and two clubs," he said. "That adds up to . . . + 100 to us, I make it."

"Must I spell it out?" said the Abbot. "I thought the double squeeze was obvious. You must keep the spades, the worthy constable must guard the clubs. Nobody, therefore, can hold on to three diamonds. Except for myself, of course."

The Inspector, who had never understood squeezes, nodded his agreement. "Had to get a full statement from you, Abbot," he said. "The er . . . double squeeze stood out a mile, as you say, but we always go through the formalities here."

The monastery team had done just enough in the final set. The match was theirs by a single-figure margin.

"Well, best of luck in your other matches," called the Inspector, as the Abbot waved farewell from the window of his dilapidated Austin Seven, ". . . to your opponents," he added under his breath.

As the car pulled out of the police yard, the Inspector could not believe his luck. "Just a minute!" he cried. "Your offside rear light's not working!"

The Abbot crunched into second gear and vanished round the corner.

"Into the Rover, lads!" cried the Inspector, making good ground across the yard.

Its siren wailing at full blast, the police car leapt forward in pursuit. "They certainly chose the wrong opponents tonight," chuckled the Inspector. "We'll have them back in those cells in no time!"